T0287750

Advance Praise for *The New Nimble*

"As the world emerges from COVID, the already rapid rate of change now seems unrelentingly faster, and its direction at any moment increasingly unclear. Through concise and accessible real-world stories, Jay Sullivan delivers thought-provoking insights and challenging inquiries to help leaders and managers navigate these uncertain times. *The New Nimble* should be required reading for business students and decision-makers at all levels of business and government."

—Bradley S. Schneider, Member of Congress, U.S. House of Representatives

"*The New Nimble* acts as a guide of resilience in the midst of extraordinary uncertainty. Jay Sullivan captures some of the most tumultuous times in human history and the many unprecedented moments that challenged all of us to find new and innovative ways to respond. At its core, it is a reassurance and an inspiration that, despite the enormity of the obstacle in our path, if we maintain proper perspective the solutions are within our grasp."

—Kathy Behrens, President – Social Responsibility & Player Programs, National Basketball Association

"Changes in demographics and attitudes toward higher education will continue to challenge college and university revenue streams for the foreseeable future. Leaders of these institutions will need to be nimble and would no doubt benefit from the insights gleaned from this book."

—Michael Lochhead, Executive Vice President – Boston College

"The world presents new challenges every day. *The New Nimble* presents a framework for preparing for and responding to those challenges effectively. Sullivan synthesizes best practices from a wide spectrum of industries, providing readers with inspiring examples of resilience as well as helpful questions to pose to our leadership teams to assess our readiness for the next seismic shift we'll undoubtedly all face."

—Henry Stoever, President & CEO – Association of Governing Boards of Universities and Colleges

"Sullivan has distilled the critical skills we all need to deal with our more uncertain and faster-changing world. In his pithy and engaging style, he has brought to life both the stories and lessons that teach us how to be "nimbler." This book could not come at a better time!"

—Robert Chen, WSJ best-selling author of *Selling Your Expertise*

"Sullivan's *New Nimble* reinforces the importance of organizational efficiency and adaptability in a variety of professional settings and industries, including higher education. As the value of advanced degrees continues to be scrutinized, institutions must learn to be nimble in a rapidly changing society. Faculty and staff in leadership roles need to read this book. It will inspire academic leaders to think critically about their organizations, learn from other industries, and develop innovative solutions to complex challenges facing the American higher education system."

—Mike Elias, Executive Director of Strategic Initiatives, University Life at the University of Pennsylvania

THE

NEW

NORMAL

MUMBLE

THE
NEW
NIMBLEORMAL

LEADING IN
THE AGE OF
CHANGE

Jay Sullivan

WILEY

Library of Congress Cataloging-in-Publication Data:

Names: Sullivan, Jay, 1962- author.
Title: The new nimble : leading in the age of change / by Jay Sullivan.
Description: Hoboken, New Jersey : Wiley, [2024] | Includes index.
Identifiers: LCCN 2023024953 (print) | LCCN 2023024954 (ebook) | ISBN 9781394185412 (hardback) | ISBN 9781394185429 (adobe pdf) | ISBN 9781394185436 (epub)
Subjects: LCSH: Organizational change. | Leadership.
Classification: LCC HD58.8 .S86 2024 (print) | LCC HD58.8 (ebook) | DDC 658.4/06—dc23/eng/20230721
LC record available at https://lccn.loc.gov/2023024953
LC ebook record available at https://lccn.loc.gov/2023024954

Cover Design Concept: Jay Sullivan

SKY10053671_082223

To Mom and Dad.

Thank you for giving me a solid, stable footing in life.

And to my children, John, Sam, Teresa, and Magdalen.

Thank you for always keeping me on my toes.

CONTENTS

Contents

Introduction: The New Nimble – Leading in the Age of Change

We're all a little bit Martha.

For more than 15 years, my wife, Mary, and I have hosted a neighborhood open-house holiday party. We missed 2019 because a family member was sick, and then 2020 because the entire world was sick. By the fall of 2021, with the hint of the world returning to normal, we decided it was time to try again.

We set the date for December 19, rented two tall space heaters for the patio so people could stay outdoors if that made them feel safer, suggested people should only come if they were vaccinated, and started making Mary's signature fudge. About a week after we mailed the invitations, Omicron reared its ugly head. As the date of the party drew closer and the news of another Covid spike grew more worrisome, a few regrets trickled in. Mary thought we should cancel the party. I wanted to move forward.

On December 16, still not sure what to do, we got a call from Martha, a sweet, elderly neighbor up the street. Martha is a wise and sound voice of reason who ran the annual science fair at the high school here in Pleasantville, New York. She and her husband, Chuck, had always attended our party and enjoyed the chance to catch up with so many people at once.

After a simple, "Hi, Mary. It's Martha." She got to the point. "I got your invitation. *ARE YOU OUT OF YOUR MINDS!*" She launched into a polite but firm tirade about the dangers of the disease, the threat to everyone right before the holidays, and the likelihood we would be hosting a super-spreader event.

Mary assured her we had space outside and that we were confident that people would only attend if they were vaccinated. In any case, Mary emphasized, we mailed the invitations before Omicron burst on the scene.

Martha shared how much she had missed seeing everyone lately, but still insisted that this was a bad idea and that we were irresponsible for moving forward with the party. She ended hurriedly with a frustrated, "Well, look, don't take us off the list because we still might come, but this is crazy," and hung up.

For three years, the entire world has been a little bit Martha, and a little bit Mary and Jay – not sure what to do, what information to weigh, what personal interests to weigh, how to make our decisions, and how to have confidence in our next steps. If we could, we delayed our decisions until we had *some* – even if not enough – information. If our decisions couldn't wait, we plowed ahead on whatever information we had. The pandemic changed so much of our lives and the way we made decisions. It forced us to abandon old ways of doing things and figure out and adopt novel approaches to connecting with each other and the various aspects of our lives.

But the pandemic only highlighted and exacerbated what's been happening in our personal and business lives for more than a decade. Those of us in leadership roles have been asked to make decisions faster, with both too much and not enough information, and with consequences that then lead to even more decisions. The only thing faster than the pace of our decisions has been the blowback from whoever didn't like the decisions. It sounds like a no-win situation. Welcome to leadership.

For the last 25+ years, I've had the privilege of both leading my own firm, and coaching business leaders on their communication skills, either in one-on-one sessions or in group classes. I have listened to thousands of professionals talk about the changes they incorporated into their work and personal lives. We've talked through how they can explain their new plans, their company's revised objectives, and their strategy for the moment, all while their situations remained in flux. We've had those conversations in the face of changing economic situations, changing regulations for their industry, and, most recently, an attack on our democracy, a war in Europe, and a global pandemic.

With each major event a company or team faced, the leader would talk about achieving a "new normal." The great frustration for everyone seemed to be that once they felt they had the situation figured out, the rules would change. They would have to start all over again. It became apparent that our "new normal" was actually all of us learning to achieve a "new nimble."

A "new normal" suggests we have achieved a new plateau, a place of stasis and stability, albeit at a place we don't really know yet. Ditch that idea. Please. We're in The New Nimble, where we will need to constantly adapt to change and to changing standards.

We've all become accustomed to making decisions in a fluid environment. The rules keep changing, the factors to consider become more complex, or, in some cases, completely out of control, and the structural underpinnings of how we think about issues no longer apply.

That shift isn't about just one aspect of our lives. It's not just about new rules about working remotely; that's just the business issue du jour. The real shift is about how business leaders are issuing "definitive" directives on Monday, and then backtracking on Tuesday because of the social media response from employees. It's about believing deeply in the stability and integrity of our democratic institutions one day and having doubts the next. It's about not just surface changes regarding how we attend meetings, but philosophical changes to how we relate to our employers and our colleagues.

In 2020, the terms *social distancing* and *essential worker* entered the world's vocabulary. Many of us, me included, humbly learned how "non-essential" the world considered us. Well prior to that, the Me Too movement and heightened awareness about racial injustice caused many of us to realize we needed to rethink our thinking – not about a particular topic, but literally about how to *think*.

We each have honed our analytic abilities from our education and life experiences. Mine come from two distinct privileges. I practiced law for nine years, first in the public interest sphere and then at a large corporate law firm. Prior to law school, I taught English grammar at a boys' high school in Kingston, Jamaica. I was able to share important grammar nuggets and my own grammar neuroses not only with my students, but to help my own four kids through high school and college. (Oddly, they were never as grateful as I would have thought.) The dual disciplines of law and grammar form the way I think through problems and structure ideas. All of the people you'll meet in this book have their own reasons for solving problems the way they do, and their own instincts for communicating their ideas for your benefit.

During Covid, many of us became more nimble in how to deal with an avalanche of work, as roles shifted and new demands arose. Others found themselves with too much time on their hands and became nimbler at finding ways to contribute to a world in pain. Regardless of which camp you found yourself in, we all needed to figure out how to be more nimble leaders in the unexpected world in which we found ourselves.

Having coached thousands of professionals dealing with an ever-changing landscape, I have observed similarities and differences in how leaders have made decisions in The New Nimble. I have gathered here the experiences of nine organizations or individuals, each from a different industry or profession. There are common elements that impact each entity's ability to succeed. There are also nuanced differences that give each unique challenges and advantages. Their experiences, insights, and innovations hold lessons for all of us as we learn to adapt, adjust, and evolve in rapidly changing times.

The "cast of characters" you'll meet on the following pages will give you insight into the specific challenges facing their industries and professions.

Universities have to adapt to new ways of teaching. But that's the least of their challenges. The remote learning model forced on us all by Covid raised questions about why we gather in person at college at all. What's the added learning we experience by coming together? Is it worth the cost? More importantly, a changing demographic in the United States will dramatically impact how universities approach recruiting and retaining students and position their value. The ivy on their walls was always taken as a sign of stability and permanence. Now, the discussions and decisions within those walls require nimble maneuvering to stay relevant and stay open.

Those in the supply chain struggle to keep our store shelves stocked and our machine parts at the ready. But pandemics, wars, and the occasional surveillance balloon disrupt supply chains or heighten concern that the links in those chains might snap.

Our product delivery systems have to work with simultaneous challenges of too much of some products and not enough of others.

The staff at hospitals and homeless shelters alike are inundated with sick and suffering sisters and brothers who need care and compassion. During the pandemic, in particular, they did so while just as frightened and uncertain as everyone else. In a world where "displaced persons" is becoming part of the demographic profile, those institutions need to adapt more nimbly than ever before. Whether your own city's downtrodden population is in need or care, or someone just bussed a few hundred homeless people to your doorstep, you're now conscious of reacting in the moment to crises that simply didn't exist a few years ago.

Consulting firms have helped their clients through industry disruptions, mergers and acquisitions, and economic uncertainty. In recent years, the pace of change has quickened, and the changes themselves have provoked fundamental existential questions for those firms and their clients alike. The world experienced a marked increase in the number of people changing jobs, employers, and even industries, causing added stress on institutions and individuals.

In the United States, our confidence in the rule of law and in the reliability of our institutions had been shaken in recent months and years. It reached a precipice on the afternoon of January 6, 2021, and shocked us all.

In the meantime, our most public of enterprises – professional sports associations – hold up the mantra of "the show must go on." But they do so on a stage that both expects but-only-sometimes welcomes their stars to weigh in on important issues of the day.

We all have our own challenges and triumphs as we navigate through an ever-changing landscape. We all figure out how to set the tone for our organizations and create new processes for dealing with crises. We each have our own failures. Our collective success will be defined by how we learn from each other's experiences. We foster creativity and innovation for ourselves and our organizations, in part, by looking beyond how our industry or company functions. I intentionally chose a diverse set of industries in the hope that successes in one field might provide inspiration for leaders in other fields.

These stories and the lessons for all of us fall into three categories.

1. Understand Your Essence,

2. Ask the Right Questions, and

3. Be Bold.

By understanding how these three elements come into play as we make decisions, we'll be better able to remain nimble both in times of crisis and in the normal levels of craziness we all experience.

Understand Your Essence

Being nimble is about being both able to pivot and knowing when to do so. We can't pivot if we don't have a starting point. Each of the organizations profiled here is highly conscious of its identity, its reason for being, and how it adds value to the world. Knowing our own essence allows us to move both deftly and strategically in a way many others cannot.

Ask the Right Questions

One of the key drivers of success during times of tumult is the right mix of confidence and humility. Without confidence, we become paralyzed. Without humility, we rush forward blindly. Humility requires accepting that we don't have all of the answers and that we need input from those around us. Asking the right questions of the right people at the right time has proven a hallmark of success for the groups you'll read about. If we put the right structures in place, we can gather the right information when we need it. If we then trust our sources, we know when to dig deeper and when to act on what's in front of us.

Be Bold

To lead, we must make decisions about our path forward and then head down that path. We have to explain those decisions to our stakeholders and accept the consequences of those decisions. The actions taken by the individuals and teams you will read about provide examples of how to engage, impact, and inspire our teams.

Throughout each chapter, I have included questions for you to consider, and approaches you and your organization could take to implement the ideas presented. This book can provide you with a guide on two levels. First, it can be your guide for assessing how your organization managed through the pandemic. Second, it can help you have the discussions that will position you well to continue to manage in a time of tumult. Ask yourself what lessons your Enterprise Risk Management group can apply as it assesses your readiness for the next unexpected upset. This is your guide for how to live in The New Nimble.

In case you are wondering, the day after Martha's call, we cancelled the party. Since we didn't have time to mail out a cancellation note, my daughters and I walked door-to-door to those families for whom we didn't have email addresses. We rang the bell, stepped back about 10 feet, and told each family the party was off. Virtually *every single neighbor* said the same thing – "Thanks for making the decision for us. We really wanted to come, but it just felt too risky." In our brief encounters, we were able to have a quick chat with each friend and catch up on how they were doing. It wasn't as much fun as a party, but on the upside, we had enough fudge to last us for weeks.

In hindsight, it was telling how many people, myself included, felt frozen about making the decision to host or attend a party. If their (my) uncertainty was so elevated regarding that simple decision, what does that suggest to all of us about deciding on all the important and complicated stuff we face each day? Fortunately, we can leverage each other's experiences and figure this out together.

I've learned a great and powerful lesson working with groups large and small in the last few years. In short, in spite of horrific behavior by some on social media, I genuinely believe we've all become more patient and forgiving in the last few years. We understand and almost welcome when a colleague's kid interrupts a Zoom meeting, or their cat walks across their computer keyboard. We're sympathetic when our meeting is interrupted because a colleague has to go sign for a delivery. We accept that you can't come to the meeting in person because earlier in the day you needed to take Dad to his doctor's appointment. The biggest and most wonderful lesson I have learned during the pandemic years working with people both remotely and now again in-person is how much more nimble we have all already become. Here are some ways to embrace and enhance that flexibility.

PART I

UNDERSTAND YOUR ESSENCE

*E*ssence is what I would call a "soft" word. It has an ephemeral quality to it. *Essence* sounds more like the name of a perfume than a business concept. And yet essence is exactly the right word to think about when it comes to the non-data, non-financial, non-legal aspects of running our enterprises.

A well-trained finance professional can look at the books of any company and figure out how the company operates. Spreadsheets vary in the details, but not in the overall construct. But looking at spreadsheets tells us little about what makes a company tick, how its leaders make decisions, how staff interacts with clients and each other, and how everyone feels about an organization. (And your stakeholders do, in fact, have feelings about your organization.) Those elements are harder to define, impossible to truly quantify regardless of any employee engagement survey, and more important to understanding how any organization – your organization – can learn to adapt to change and be nimble in the moment.

To help you reflect on the essence of your organization, we'll look at three organizations and how their response to the pandemic was driven by their essence. To be self-aware as a company you need to know your purpose as an entity, the values that drive that purpose, and the limits of your control over your circumstances. It's not just about being conscious about these elements of your business. It's about inhaling and exhaling them with every breath at work. Like an athlete in "the zone" who performs with more agility, you and your organization can respond more nimbly if you know and live your essence.

CHAPTER 1

Know Yourself (and Let Others Know You, Too)

Having coached people for more than 25 years, I've often reminded my clients of the old adage, "The only person's behavior you can control is your own." You can't make other people do something they don't want to do. All you can do is change the way you interact with them to see if you can get a different response from them.

You can't control how other people might ask you to change, that is, be nimble. But if you know with conviction what you stand for, what you will and won't do, then when others expect you to flex in the moment to accomplish a goal, you'll know the extent to which you will bend and accommodate. You'll also know what's outside of your boundaries. If other people know who you are and how you approach the world, they'll know intrinsically what they can ask of you. If your personal brand is unclear, or if other people don't know you, their demands on you to be more nimble and adjust your approach may seem, well, unseemly. Their requests will appear too demanding, or just inconsistent with how you are capable of adjusting.

The same is true on an institutional level. If people both inside and outside your organization know who you are and what you believe, they have a sense of your parameters for your behavior. They then target their requests and demands accordingly.

As a result, it becomes easier for you to adjust on the fly, respond to crises, and manage the demands likely to come your way. Knowing your purpose, understanding your motivation, and articulating your boundaries will help you be more nimble as the need arises.

PROFILE: COVENANT HOUSE (NON-PROFITS) – "YOUR MISSION BRINGS YOU MIRACLES"

I graduated from Fordham Law School in 1989 at the height of the AIDS (acquired immunodeficiency syndrome) epidemic. Because of a generous fellowship program from the Skadden Foundation, I was able to accept a role as in-house counsel at Covenant House, a shelter for young people facing homelessness. Covenant House has always identified its facilities as "crisis shelters" since the young people who come to the agency are in crisis. They have nowhere else to go and no one else to turn to.

At the time, the agency was operated out of a converted detention facility a few blocks west of the Port Authority bus terminal in Manhattan. Covenant House had the only residential unit in the country specifically designed for HIV (human immunodeficiency virus)-positive young people. For two years, my job was to represent those young people on AIDS-related discrimination issues they were facing, and, because it was AIDS in the 1980s, to help them write their wills. In addition to serving teenagers with HIV, I counseled all of the residents in the agency on whatever legal issues arose.

AIDS was the leprosy of its generation. Homeless youth live every day as outcasts already. Adding an HIV+ diagnosis to their already fragile existence was like putting a hurdle on a track already covered in shards of glass. Covenant House rose to the challenge and managed to provide a community to a most desperate population. I knew the agency's ability to think creatively in times of crisis and to react consistent with its mission. I wondered how it responded to the many variables we've all faced in the last few years.

As Covid exploded into our lives and infiltrated our psyches in 2020, Covenant House was operating in cities in the United States and Canada, and with homes for street children in Mexico, Guatemala, and Nicaragua. A staff of 2,200 served more than 2,000 young people every night. The staff's mission was simple – to serve youth in need. And their ethos – to act with unconditional love and absolute respect – has never changed and is understood and voiced in actions large and small by every staff member.

Sr. Nancy Downing became the Executive Director of Covenant House New York in 2016. Prior to that role, she served as the agency's Director of Advocacy and Legal Services, and as General Counsel for Covenant House International (CHI). She was sitting at her desk on the eighth floor in the New York shelter in early March 2020 when she received word from the city's health department. "Congregate care" facilities like Covenant House would have to institute social distancing policies to limit the spread of Covid. The shelter would have to reduce the number of young people already in the building and close its intake. Sr. Nancy, as everyone called her, knew if the agency turned away kids arriving at the door seeking help, those young people would likely sleep on the floor of Port Authority or Penn Station or engage in some dangerous and destructive behavior that would advance a downward spiral. The agency had never closed its doors to youth in need in the 50-plus years since its founding. She slumped at her desk with her head in her hands, sighing deeply.

In addition to a law degree, Sr. Nancy holds a BA in criminal justice, a certificate in pastoral studies, and a certificate in non-profit management from Columbia Business School. In other words, she has grounding in method, mission, and momentum. She doesn't sit still for long. She gave herself two minutes of self-pity and despair. She sat back in her chair, wondering how a crisis-shelter agency should respond in this moment of its own crisis.

Sr. Nancy contemplated the "question presented," the language lawyers use when articulating the challenge we're asked to tackle. That night close to 300 young adults would be sleeping in Covenant House sites in New York City, many in rooms of three to four people each. Telling any of those individuals they had to leave was not an option, nor was turning away any other young person who arrived in need. Sr. Nancy had to follow the rules. She also had to live the agency's mission. And she had to act, and quickly.

When we solve problems, we don't start at the macro level. We start with what's right in front of us. "We had to create more space so we could spread out the residents," she said. She looked around her office and something clicked. "I thought, 'We need to fit a bed in this room.'" After a quick meeting with her leadership team to gain agreement, she dragged the chairs and small table from her office into the hallway and turned her desk to face the wall. Her colleagues did likewise. The maintenance staff pulled extra beds from storage.

Because the agency was housed in a former detention facility, each office had a small bathroom, so each could serve as a room for one or two residents. Within days, they had cleared 18 offices of files, computers, and paperwork. They dragged whatever they could to the conference room. A few weeks later, the piles in the conference room would also include boxes of personal protection equipment (PPE) and other Covid-related supplies.

Ultimately, Covenant House would not have to turn away any kid in need, not in New York or Anchorage or Fort Lauderdale or Toronto, or any of the other 30 facilities. Every person I spoke with at the agency highlighted with both tremendous pride and tremendous relief, "We never closed our doors." Knowing your mission gives you focus. Believing in the importance of your mission generates the creativity needed to be nimble in the moment.

Because Sr. Nancy knew the parameters of the organization – never turn a kid away – she was able to take that option off the table and focus on other solutions.

At the start of Covid, Covenant House New York, had already started building a new facility on an adjacent site. It was to be the agency's first purpose-built shelter in New York. The agency had 50 years of experience understanding what might work best for a crisis shelter. The timing of the build-out allowed it to leverage the lessons of Covid into the new design. Constructing individual bathrooms rather than dormitory style set-ups was one key development.

According to Deirdre Cronin, then the Chief Operation Officer at CHI, the shelters operate independently, but provide a ready-made network of ideas and inspiration for each other. That network became invaluable during the pandemic, as the issues the shelters faced became ever more complex. They set up an Emergency Response Working Group (ERWG) that included at least one person from each site. The group met weekly, leveraging each other's experiences. In addition, the group had the subject matter expertise of Dr. Michael Dean, who had been on the agency's Board of Trustees. Dr. Dean distilled and deciphered the vast amount of information and sometimes conflicting recommendations coming from various medical sources.

The first priority at each shelter was to revamp the intake process. The agency had to protect the health and safety of its staff and the current residents. The state had provided a series of questions to ask people seeking shelter regarding their potential exposure to Covid.

Are you experiencing any of the following symptoms?

Have you been diagnosed with Covid?

Have you been exposed to anyone who has been diagnosed with Covid?

Those questions weren't going to mean much for the young people coming through Covenant House's intake process. When you are trying to come in out of the cold, and when you have spent your life in survival mode, you learn to answer questions not based on the truth but based on the version of the truth that will get you what you need, in this case, shelter. The Covenant House intake team learned to listen differently than others might have in an effort to meet the mission of the organization.

According to Alison Kear, the Executive Director of Covenant House Anchorage, "We needed to communicate to young people seeking shelter, 'We know you have Covid. Come in anyway.'" During Covid, the streets of Anchorage, previously dotted with small groups of homeless young people standing on street corners, became ghost towns. But they were empty not because those young people went into hiding. They were empty because the kids found a place of safety.

Once the agency knew it could continue to service its population, the attention to minutia took over. "We needed PPE, but we didn't know what that meant," Cronin said. "We thought we needed gowns, gloves, goggles, masks, and thermometers. We were scrambling to find all of this stuff at the same time as everyone else. I met with my team of 10 and we decided to all go on Amazon at midnight to buy N95 masks, thinking no one else would have the same idea. Apparently, it was a great idea because so many other people had the same idea that the sites were jammed. We had to pivot." (Cronin noted that during the pandemic she grew weary of two phrases: "We need to pivot" and "Let's stick a pin in that for the moment.") "We have a few staff members that live in western New Jersey, near the border with Pennsylvania," Cronin recalled. "They drove to their local Target to buy rain ponchos to wear as protective gowns. We were trying to think of anything we could do to meet the demands and keep everyone safe."

Covenant House is funded primarily by donations from individuals and foundations. It has a devoted donor group. Cronin noted that most of the time agencies need to reach out to donors for support. Throughout the first year of the pandemic, donors were calling the agency to see how they could help. When it was evident that masks were hard to come by, donors started sewing masks by hand and shipping them to the agency. Because only essential childcare workers were allowed at the shelter, Cronin asked donors to ship the masks directly to her home. She then enlisted friends and her kids' Confirmation classes to help her repackage literally thousands of masks and shipped them to the various shelters. "Being nimble for us meant calling on all of our resources and stakeholders – our staff, our board members, our donors, state and local governments – you name it," Cronin said.

Again, because the donor population knew the agency well and felt a connection to the agency, donors knew the place couldn't and wouldn't shut its doors, and therefore would need help.

MASKING YOUR FACE, NOT YOUR FEELINGS

Providing shelter proved to be the easiest part of meeting the needs of the population Covenant House served. Sr. Nancy shared, "Our young people have faced so many obstacles in life all alone. They didn't have the support of their families the way most of us did. Their frame of reference is one of isolation and desperation. We had always been able to alleviate that for them by giving them a sense of community and someone to talk to. Now they were coming to us, and we were telling them they had to stay in their rooms and avoid contact with each other and staff, the antithesis of community."

According to Cronin, the Covenant House model is to get young people experiencing homelessness off the street; take care of their immediate needs like food, rest, shelter, and clean clothes; and then get them on a plan. They should be out looking for work, looking for permanent housing, applying to a job training program. We're always thinking about how to stabilize their lives and get them ready to take care of themselves. Cronin said, "In Covid, the plan narrowed to simply staying safe. There were no jobs to be had, and other avenues where on hold. Suddenly, we had the kids in the shelter 24/7, which is not the norm for us."

"To keep them engaged and alleviate some of the anxiety, we did things for them we had never done before," Sr. Nancy noted. "We had always encouraged residents to get together in small groups to talk. Conversations build relationships, and relationships are the best antidote to isolation and depression." Now, the biggest challenge for the staff was helping the kids fight boredom, the kind of boredom that might prompt them to leave the agency, risk exposure, and return to the residence and infect others.

The agency bought iPads and Netflix subscriptions. They brought in food they had never served before. When your default for feeding a few hundred people is a cafeteria model, which is inherently unsafe in a pandemic, the staff had to rethink how to get kids their meals. The focus was on keeping the residents settled and safe and solitary.

Renee Trincanello manages the Covenant House operations in Fort Lauderdale and Orlando, Florida. For her, communicating the constant changes in protocol was essential. "In times like this," she noted, "You think you've reached the hardest point in dealing with crisis and then something else happens." There was a tremendous amount of misinformation flying around. To reduce the level of chaos for the staff and residents, she based her decisions on three sources of information: the Centers for Disease Control and Prevention (CDC), the Florida State Board of Education, and Dr. Dean of CHI.

By narrowing her sources, she and her team were able to synthesize information and reach conclusions efficiently. One challenge Trincanello faced that the other Covenant House locations did not have to address was the discrepancy between the agency's directives and state mandates. CHI decided to mandate vaccinations for all employees. The State of Florida threatened sanctions against any employer that did so. Trincanello reached a "happy medium": she would mandate masks and encourage vaccinations. In the end, 60% of Florida staff got vaccinated.

"In Alaska," Kear notes, "we always feel like we are about two weeks behind the rest of the country on lots of levels. In our Covid response, we would have been a full month behind if I hadn't had the Covenant House ERWG." Apparently, no one in social services in Anchorage was expressing urgency around the pandemic just yet.

One of the crucial elements of becoming more innovative is to network both within your industry and discipline, and among others who may think differently or have a different approach to solving problems.[1] "I was meeting frequently with the executive directors of the other shelters. My team was treating this as something abstract and in the future. New York was dealing with it in real time, in very concrete terms," Kear noted. "As a result, I was not only able to put a plan in place for our shelter, but I also actually shared our plan with the city of Anchorage to help them prepare for what was to come."

Anchorage was less at risk than major cities because it doesn't have a huge mass transit system or other factors that concentrate a lot of people into a small space. However, the city was at risk from another angle. Kear notes, "We only have one large hospital for an enormous geographic region. If our local hospital became overrun, we'd have major problems. The ability to learn what other groups were doing was essential both to get the information to us, and to help us get it to others."

To truly become innovative, which allows us to be more nimble as needed, we're better off if we network outside our closest community. The leadership teams at the various Covenant House sites were able to network not just among themselves, but with other social service providers in their local communities. In addition, for years Kear had attended a variety of conferences across the country to gain exposure to other groups.

DEEPER CHALLENGES AND BROADER OPPORTUNITIES

"These young people have been through so much in their short lives," Sr. Nancy notes. "Some residents in our longer-term programs have achieved a sense of structure and stability for the first time in their lives. Helping the residents battle despair became a primary focus for the staff." Sr. Nancy recounted, "I was in the elevator with one young man one day in April. He had recently landed a great job and was feeling really good about himself. Then Covid hit. He shared with me that he had just lost his job and he burst into tears. Everything had been a mess before. He had fought so hard to get where he was and now it was all gone again."

"I realized we needed to look beyond the immediate. The pandemic wouldn't last forever. When we came out of this, we needed to make sure our young people had a fighting chance." She recounted that when the financial crisis of 2008 hit, most of the kids not only lost their jobs, but were also at the back of the line to get rehired.

"Our CovWorks career counseling staff worked to make sure that when the economy came back, the Covenant House residents didn't get left behind. Staff talked to employers about what jobs they thought would be needed and pivoted in-house training programs accordingly.

Often, crises present opportunities. This was true especially for Covenant House Alaska. Sixty percent of the agency's Anchorage residents are Alaskan Natives. One-third of young homeless people in Anchorage come from the small town of Bethel, Alaska, a town of only 4,000.

When the federal government offered relief packages, the Alaskan tribal entities were not eligible. The tribes joined in a lawsuit, which Covenant House Alaska also supported, seeking inclusion. Through various programs, the tribes became eligible for $450 million in federal relief. The only stipulation was that the money had to be spent in six months. Organizations applying for the relief had to guarantee they could implement and complete a project in that amount of time. When the funds became available, Kear was at a hospital in Florida caring for her step-father who was dying of cancer. Via Zoom, she negotiated with four tribes to fund two long-term projects her team had designed and for which they had been looking for funding – Covey Lofts and Covey Academy.

Kear bought the building behind the agency's shelter and converted it into Covey Lofts, 24 efficiency apartments. Those units provide long-term shelter for residents to get them off the street, stabilized, and able to move on to a more long-term situation. She listened to the needs and wish lists of the residents. They wanted locks on the door to feel a sense of ownership and privacy, and their own thermostat, to literally control their own environment, both reasonable requests. They didn't want the responsibility of their own kitchen in their apartment; they just needed a microwave, but a communal kitchen on the first floor they could use when they wanted to. This was fortuitous since it simplified construction, a crucial factor when operating on a tight deadline. Listening to the needs of the population being served actually enabled Kear to meet the parameters around the funding.

The four Alaska Native tribes also funded Covey Academy, which allowed the agency to develop training programs around specific jobs needed in rural Alaska. The program helps residents get their commercial driver's license, learn to operate heavy equipment, work in road construction, and even get their pilot's license.

Because the funding became available, Covenant House Alaska was also able to create pilot programs to provide social services in Bethel to stem the flow of young people from that community.

"Mission" Is Mission-Critical

Kear is quick to point out that one reason her team was successful at leveraging the opportunities presented during the pandemic was because the organization stayed true to its mission. She was conscious of not falling prey to what she calls "mission-drift." "We're a shelter for young people in need. They need housing, job training, and life skills. All of our development plans stayed true to that mission. When funds became available, we didn't run out and open a restaurant or something else outside our focus or expertise. Because we know who we are and why we exist, we were successful. Our team really showed its mettle. It's a fantastic group of professionals. Covenant House Alaska came through the last two years much stronger than before."

Louis Pasteur is quoted as having said, "Fortune favors the prepared mind." Kear would add a theological spin to Pasteur's quote: "Your mission brings you miracles."

While miracles do happen, they aren't a game plan for most successful businesses. The leadership team at Covenant House credits staff, donors, and miracles with much of its ability to not only survive but thrive during the pandemic. In truth, the team's hard work, preparation, and diligence drove much of its success.

From a leadership perspective, it was important to live the mission not only for the residents, but for the staff. "Our people are tremendously dedicated. But like everyone else, they were also scared and pulled in many directions," Sr. Nancy noted. "At one point someone asked me if I was frightened or concerned for my health. I told them of course I was, but the kids still needed to be served." When the agency had to put an entire floor of residents into isolation, Sr. Nancy took one of the first overnight shifts. "I couldn't ask the staff to take on a heavy burden like that if I wasn't willing to do so myself," she said. "Besides," she said, chuckling, "I didn't have an office anymore. I was operating out of a small corner in someone else's space."

Kear, in Alaska, believes firmly that showing your staff members that you are investing in them and their well-being makes an enormous difference. And it starts at the top. When the pandemic first hit, Kear knew the organization would have trouble keeping the donation money coming in, since its regular fundraising events had to be cancelled. "It was a huge relief when CHI called the first week of shutdown to say it would cover two payroll cycles," she said. Although we operate mostly independently, the Covenant House network supports each other tremendously."

Kear hired wellness coaches for her team to suggest how they can take care of themselves so they can show up and take care of others. And she knew she had to set an example for them. "Your people need to see you taking care of your own physical and mental well-being," she notes. Prior to the pandemic, Kear had been a road warrior. In addition to traveling for conferences, for two years before the pandemic, Kear was an Annie E. Casey Fellow, which required her to fly from Anchorage to Baltimore every six weeks for leadership training. Quoting flight attendants, she advises, "Put on your own oxygen mask before helping others."

Sometimes the identification with mission can hurt you if you aren't careful about how it's messaged to others. When the pandemic first hit, the City of Anchorage made funding available for other organizations to open shelters. When Kear asked about funding for her agency the response was, in essence, "We don't need to fund your shelter. That's your mission." Kear shared with local authorities how, by taking homeless young people off the street and helping them stabilize, they are decreasing the future adult homeless population. Through a combination of data and passion she turned around their initial skepticism about supporting the agency. Now, a significant portion of the organization's core programming is funded through a local alcohol tax, a change Kear never imagined.

Throughout my conversations with the team at Covenant House, the focus always came back to how proud they were that the agency never closed its doors or turned away a kid in need. Employees know their mission. Very often, an organization's mission is proudly displayed on a wall in a reception area. At Covenant House, it's not only on the wall, it's in the very vibe of the place and in the virtues shown in the way the staff addresses the individuals it serves. The catchphrase "unconditional love and absolute respect" comes up time and again. Keeping that mission front and center for each individual allowed the organization to stay focused and deliver in a time of great uncertainty.

TAKEAWAYS

I have worked with many corporate entities on team-building initiatives and communication challenges. I can attest that at many places the staff passes by the mission statement on the wall, but can't recite it, or, more importantly, articulate the "why" behind the statement. We're heading down a path where stakeholders demand two contradictory behaviors from us. First, they want decisions to be supported by data. We need empirical evidence that our position is sound, and our goals will be achieved. Second, they want decisions faster, which seems counter to being able to support decisions with thoughtful analysis and data. As we're required to be more nimble, we can increase our likelihood of success on both fronts if we keep our mission at the forefront of our discernment process.

How can you help yourself and your team accomplish this goal?

Set aside time at your next strategic planning meeting to discuss the mission of the organization. Don't just have people recite the mission. Have them privately, on paper, note their understanding of the "why" behind the mission. Ask them to articulate why that mission is important:

- to the organization as a whole,
- to the business unit they operate,
- to their immediate team, and
- to them personally.

The "why" of the mission will and should change as it goes from being more abstract on the larger level to more concrete and personal for each individual. It's important that you have everyone privately write down their responses to these questions. You want to understand their perspective before it's influenced by the language and delivery of their peers. Once everyone has committed their ideas on paper, have them share aloud or in small groups how they frame the answers to these questions. Now comes your analysis.

First, note how consistent or diverse the responses are to the "why" of the mission on the grand enterprise-wide level. If the responses from your team are fairly consistent, you're in good shape. If there is a lack of consistency, you may need to regroup and re-discuss how people view the organization. You won't be able to nimbly maneuver the ship through the next storm if the group isn't in agreement on why they're heading in a certain direction.

Second, note how your team members incorporate that broader mission into the work of their own business units. Does their translation of that mission surprise you? Make sense to you? Help you understand why they function as well as they do or fit into the bigger picture the way they do?

Finally, articulating for yourself how the mission of the organization helps you show up at work each morning with your full energy and "best self" will inform for you your own motivation at work. Understanding how that motivation drives each of your direct reports will help you know how to guide them in their decision-making as we are called on to shift priorities, consider alternative perspectives, and react quickly to changing circumstances.

If you're good at what you do, those you serve will always ask you to do more. They'll see you as a broader resource than how you usually position yourself. That's a good thing. Have you ever had a client call you and say, "I'm not sure this is something you do, but…." Or "I know this is a bit outside your regular wheelhouse, but would you consider doing…?" It's flattering when clients ask those questions. It means you've done a great job positioning yourself as just a smart person and good business partner, able to help in many ways. Those questions don't drag you into the realm of "mission-drift." They simply give you an opportunity to consider whether the request is part of your mission and therefore skill set, or too far afield. Then, you can decide whether to accept the new opportunity, or decline it. I have handled many such questions and responded sometimes with, "Glad to discuss how we can help," and sometimes with, "Not our area of expertise, but I'm glad to refer you to people I know who can help."

Our mission defines how we add value to the world. Our understanding of the elasticity in that mission allows us to be nimble in our ever-evolving work lives.

Questions for you and your team to consider:

How do our stakeholders view us? Do they know intrinsically what we do, what we're willing to try, and what is absolutely off the table?

Does our internal team know the same?

What are the natural affinity groups within which we network?

What other groups could we connect with or expose ourselves to in order to gain a broader perspective?

When we create our strategic plan, how much wiggle room do we include?

If opportunities presented themselves, how quickly could we advance – or delay – the timeline as needed?

Did we build that flexibility into the process?

CHAPTER 2

Be Your Better Self

In Chapter 1 we looked at the "why" behind the "what" for an organization. The "why" for most for-profit enterprises is evident from that very name – they exist "for profit." If a business isn't making money, it doesn't last long. Even the most enticing internet startup has to eventually demonstrate how it can monetize its services or it doesn't last. And non-profits need to demonstrate value, or they cease to gain the widespread public support to fund their operations.

But the essence of an organization isn't limited to its mission and the motivation for that mission. It also includes the way people act while executing on that mission. We all spend more time doing our jobs than doing any other single activity in our daily lives. We brainstorm solutions with each other, mentor and develop newer team members, and execute on our tasks. How we treat our colleagues and clients engaging in these activities defines a large part of our organization's essence.

The guidelines underpinning our interactions might be listed in an employee code of conduct. However, our actions on any given day, in any given interaction are likely influenced more immediately by the values our organization claims to profess. An organization's values are not usually handed down from the top, although they may have originated from the personality of the organization's founder. More likely, they grow from the body of staff members, and they create that company's culture.

Culture evolves slowly but can change abruptly under new leadership. When a new teacher enters the classroom, the culture of the class changes. When divisions merge, two groups of people are wary at first about how to approach each other. I have worked with many teams that had been combined either from different organizations or various parts of the same organization. People in those groups hang on to their professional "upbringing," claiming their background as "legacy X" or "legacy Y," either out of pride or to make excuses for bad behavior, or sometimes both.

Culture can also be impacted by a decision by leadership that is inconsistent with the values of the organization. If our employees or customers see us acting at odds with those values, we lose credibility.

Our culture, as defined by our values, either allows us to move swiftly in a time of upheaval or gets in the way. It's important to consider the values we possess as we look at making decisions in a more nimble fashion.

PROFILE: BOWERY FARMING (SUSTAINABILITY) – LET YOUR VALUES GUIDE YOU

"The pandemic forced companies to move from *talking about* what they can do to *proving they can do it*," says Caralyn Cooley, Chief People Officer at Bowery Farming.

Cultures evolve over time but can be undermined quickly if not nurtured. Agriculture is as old as civilization, and, apparently, as new as the latest software program coming out of a young and fast-growing "vertical farming" company. Bowery Farming, only five years old when the pandemic struck, is bringing large-scale farming to the great indoors. Its ability to have managed through the pandemic depended on both a dogged attachment to its core values and on a nimbleness to figure out how to stay true to those values in a rapidly evolving landscape.

When we think of corporate visionaries, we think of Richard Branson or Marc Benioff. When we think of industry disrupters, we think of tech or media companies such as Airbnb or Napster. We don't think of farmers, and we don't think of crop yields. We think of farming as stable, static, and about as much fun as watching grass grow. In a world of online ordering, instant messaging, and constant streaming, how could monitoring kale and parsley seedlings require quick action, creative responses, and nimbleness? Apparently, quite a bit.

Every organization has its guiding principles, its own ethos, its unique statement of its reason for being. Those of us in leadership roles at our firms found ourselves grappling daily with how to use the "North Star" of our values to drive our decisions. We did so even when it would have been easy to abandon principles in favor of economics and expedience. Bowery Farming's values took even stronger root during the pandemic, and helped the firm both grow and blossom. (*Warning:* There will be lots of unapologetic plant, farming, soil, and weather metaphors in this chapter.)

Caralyn Cooley, Bowery's Chief People Officer, joined the company one year before the pandemic. In her 20 years as a human resources professional, she has worked at Pepsi, Amazon, and Nordeus, a mobile game manufacturer. She has worked for large, global companies, as well as small, local entities, and understands how culture impacts both.

Bowery exists "to grow food smarter for more people in more places." That's its mission. In the last chapter, we talked about the importance of people owning the mission of the organization in order to stay focused. You can't help but think about Bowery's slogan, "farming from the ground up" when you stand inside one of Bowery's vertical farms. Your eye is naturally drawn upward to the stacks of trays soaring into the rafters, each blooming with seedlings. The smell is earthy and stable, but the view is heavenward and futuristic.

Agriculture will need to become more sustainable if we are going to feed the 10 billion people who will inhabit the planet in 2050. Part of that sustainability means moving food production closer to the urban areas where most of the population will live, reducing transportation time and improving the freshness of produce. Bowery's "constant improvement" focus requires all hands, heads, and hearts to stay in the conversation.

In 2019, Glassdoor, the website that gathers and shares information on employee satisfaction, surveyed visitors on the importance of culture and values when applying for a job. More than 79% of respondents indicated that they would consider a company's mission and purpose before applying for a job. Seventy-three percent said they wouldn't apply to a company unless its values aligned with their own. Finally, millennials listed an employer's culture and values as more important factors than salary. This information suggests that attracting new talent, which equates with attracting new ideas, requires a very clear statement about your company's culture and values.

A look at Bowery's four driving values and how each played into its ability to remain nimble can be instructive for all leaders.

VALUE #1 – OPT IN

Bowery defies being categorized. It's a tech company, creating both hardware and software products. It's a manufacturing company since it grows food. It's a branded consumer packaged goods (CPG) company that sells to retailers. Its science arm oversees research and development (R&D) and product development. Maintaining such a complex identity in such a small company requires intense collaboration.

At many early-stage companies, senior leaders often wear many hats; everyone pitches in. Cooley shared, "When you're growing as a company, you design roles around the people on board and the skills they have." The second employee at Bowery was Dr. Henry Sztul, who conceived of some of the company's core concepts and ran the experiments to determine the viability of Bowery's approach. Because Sztul was always willing to step in where needed, he added the company's technology needs to his portfolio. As the company grew and both the science and tech needs expanded, the company split the two functions and created teams around each. Sztul became the Chief Science Officer, and the firm brought in a dedicated Chief Technology Officer.

That kind of adaptation is essential and typical of most companies as they evolve. In times of rapid change, the attitude that "we're all in this together" is essential. That can mean returning to the more nimble instincts of a startup. At Bowery, that multiple-role concept carried throughout all levels, as no task was too small or too big. During the pandemic, this meant radical reassignment. The bookkeeping staff didn't just have to now work to support another corporate function; it had to cover shifts in the farm. When the corporate-types at Bowery reference getting out of the C-Suite and "getting their hands dirty" or "getting down in the weeds," on projects, they aren't speaking metaphorically.

On more than a few occasions, Chief People Officer Cooley found herself working in the farm alongside – but six feet apart from – one of the company's software engineers, a marketing manager, and a recruiter, all just getting the job done. While she spends most days helping people grow their skills and consider the next step in their professional evolution, her time on the farm gave her the chance to do the same for the company's produce, replanting arugula and dandelion greens seedlings from their initial trays into larger "rafts." The willingness, and even eagerness to do so, is a hallmark of the company's success.

VALUE #2 – THINK WILDLY DIFFERENT

When your mission is to reinvent the agricultural industry from top to bottom, you have to be willing to rethink every element of your business world. If your company is considered a disrupter in your industry, you'll be familiar with this matrix thinking to solving problems.

For Bowery, solving the agricultural challenge the world is facing means looking at water usage, transportation issues, the impact of global climate change on how plant species thrive or die, and getting healthy food to diverse communities on a more equitable basis. No small feat.

More than 85% of the company's employees joined since the start of the pandemic. As an HR professional, Cooley had to think differently about how to create engagement with that group and instill the company's culture for them.

Bowery considers itself an in-person company. It's crucial to the culture it has created.

"It was a huge decision on March 12 [2020], to shut HQ for two weeks," Cooley said. "We had to be incredibly flexible when making decisions since the guidance coming into the organization kept changing. "Initially, research showed that wearing masks made the situation worse. Two weeks later, they were required. Every decision felt like 'two steps forward; one step back.'"

Because Bowery was still an early-stage company, even prior to the shutdown, Irving Fain, Bowery's Founder and CEO, conducted "all-hands" meetings every three weeks. Once Covid started, Fain held these sessions every week to maintain a sense of connectedness. To combat the isolation people were feeling, he added email updates twice a week. This lasted for a year.

But the camaraderie that people felt meeting every week was too important to abandon. So, to give people more frequent opportunities to connect on the weeks between Fain's meetings, Cooley organized social connections such as company-wide Zoom Happy Hours. "It was a nice effort, but they lost their appeal very quickly. We needed something else. We had an amazing culture that was welcoming and creative. We didn't want to lose that."

Cooley's team had to be creative and flexible, so they brainstormed ideas for how to keep people connected. They decided to try a series of training programs. "We ran all sorts of training sessions on things like communication skills, health and wellness, and financial literacy. Those worked very well." But they had to keep producing new topics. (At the end of this chapter, I've provided some guidance on how to brainstorm new ideas with your team.)

After a year, Fain's bi-weekly emails were reduced to once per week, and then on an as-needed basis. The all-hands meetings decreased in frequency as well. However, the regular team training offerings continued for two years. Remaining nimble means getting comfortable with a "trial and error" approach. When you are trying to become nimbler in your decision-making, you need to get more comfortable with efforts that don't work. Evaluate *why* an initiative didn't work, and decide if structurally, it wasn't the right fix, or if the timing was just off. In a rapidly changing environment, a failed attempt one month might be just the right fix a few months later.

According to Cooley, there are many paths forward in any situation. The important part is to just get moving. "Getting ahead by getting started" became a common mantra for her team.

As difficult situations drag on, we need to adapt our approaches. Early in the pandemic, Bowery's team issued new protocols with the caveat that they were, "written in pencil, not pen." While that was helpful at first, after a few months the group needed more stability in decisions, and the expression was considered "overused." Any organization's rules and regulations need to exist somewhere between "carved in stone," and "subject to change on a moment's notice."

"Bowery always had flexibility in its DNA," Cooley said, "but didn't always have to use it." The pandemic changed that. The company had to be comfortable evolving. Some of its team of 650 people managed large-scale, indoor, multilevel vertical farms. Others wrote computer code, creating the BoweryOS, an operating system in place at all of Bowery's farms. That same team implemented software that tracked the health of the crops and allowed the company to make decisions about crop care. All employees needed to deal with substantive change on a daily basis. On any given day, you didn't know who from the shift you managed would call in sick. You didn't know what new functionality someone would ask you to create in one of the software packages. The list of "You didn't knows" was endless. It required a more nuanced and nimble response.

Cooley notes, "I thrive in uncertainty and always try to stay optimistic. When we face a new challenge, at first, I don't know how we will figure it out, but I'm always confident that we will." That openness to trying new things and being willing to fail at some efforts is very empowering to teams.

Cooley found that open approach to be true not just within Bowery, but in her wider network as well. As a member of a number of both casual and formal "Chief People Officer" networks, she attended regular discussions during the pandemic where people shared best practices. In some environments, she indicated, some people would have kept their best ideas to themselves to give them a competitive advantage in the war for talent. During Covid, she felt her peers in the world of HR were incredibly open and happy to share ideas, knowing that, in some ways, we were all in this pandemic together and needed all the good ideas we could get.

VALUE #3 – BREAK BARRIERS TOGETHER

Pre-Covid, Bowery's culture had always been full-time in the office. That constant physical presence was important to their culture. A majority of employees went to the office and the farms every day. You can't do R&D from home. You can't "break barriers *together*" when you're alone. "Our business is highly cross-functional and requires extensive collaboration across teams and functions," Cooley says. "We're constantly innovating. We have found that innovation activities like brainstorming, building prototypes, and piloting new ideas move faster and more effectively in person. Collaborating with people in person is also tremendously helpful to building trust.

Bowery sees itself as an innovation company. According to Cooley, "speed is one of the most important things about innovating, and being together helps us move ideas forward and implement them faster." While teams have worked remotely for decades, the consensus at Bowery is that its team members work more efficiently when they can be physically present with each other.

Two weeks before the Covid shut-down, senior leadership started discussing how the pandemic could impact them. Given the social-distancing restrictions, the leadership knew it would have to be creative in its approach to staffing.

They divided the employees into three categories.

1. People who had to go to the facilities every day, such as the farm workers.

2. People who could feasibly work from home, such as marketing managers.

3. People who could do some portions of their work from home, but otherwise needed to be in-person, such as the design engineers.

The "nimbleness" came into play in the speed with which they made these decisions and categorized every employee in the company. "I think it took about 24 hours from concept to communication," Cooley said. "Fain and I made the initial assessments, and then did a quick gut check with the Leadership Team." Flexibility came into play as they realized that roles that could function remotely for two weeks weren't handled effectively that way long term. As the pandemic progressed, everyone at Bowery ended up in employee category 1 or 3; the nature of the company – and the values of the organization – required the collaboration that only happens when people are face-to-face.

If we are independent contributors at our organization, our individual behavior impacts only us. If we skip the party or the meeting, we're the ones who lose out. However, when you are a leader, your behavior sets the tone for the entire organization. Line professionals take their lead on how to act by watching the more experienced members of their team. There's a strong belief at Bowery that if a more-senior person doesn't show up at an event or for in-person meetings, they aren't the only ones who suffer a loss. If the leader doesn't show, the whole group loses out.

For Bowery to remain innovative, Cooley's team needed to figure out how to collaborate at a distance. They tried numerous combinations of meeting frequencies, durations, and combinations of participants before settling on a pattern that worked. Being nimble meant being open to a variety of ideas in order to solve the problem.

Some companies readily admit they didn't see the pandemic coming and hadn't prepared for it, even though they had well-developed crisis plans for other natural disasters. At Bowery, in late 2019, as news of a unique virus was spreading in Asia, Bowery's leadership team discussed the avian bird flu and how its then-employers had responded. Spotting the issue even just a few months before it was on the company's doorstep gave Bowery time to develop continuity protocols in the event of a pandemic. The company had a Slack channel in place and a phone-tree protocol for getting the word out about any Covid emergencies.

VALUE #4 – BE KIND TO THE CORE

In the well-known Maslow's Hierarchy of Needs, after our physiological needs for food, water, and shelter, our next essential needs are for different elements of safety. "Safety" includes our personal security, employment, resources, property, and health. Covid threatened all five of these needs. We didn't know our risk for infection or the likely severity of the impact if we contracted the disease. Many people were at risk for and did, in fact, lose their jobs because of the shutdown. Even if we maintained our employment, the overall level of our income was in question. We were rightly worried on many levels.

According to Cooley, at the outset of the pandemic, a huge portion of her workforce was simply scared. What allowed Bowery to be nimble in its response to those fears was to rely on its core principle of being "kind to the core."

When we put other people first, we think about the impact of our actions on their psyche. We protect them on many levels, which allows them to continue functioning. Cooley and her team knew they needed to act quickly to demonstrate this value in action. They immediately started organizing small-group meetings where people could share their concerns and frustrations.

The health and safety concerns impacted various groups of employees differently. To understand those unique challenges each group faced, Cooley and her team would begin each small group meeting by asking, "What's making you uncomfortable and scared?" The results differed drastically.

Those on the farms voiced concerns about masks and social distancing. Rules regarding both differed in Pennsylvania, Maryland, and New Jersey, three of the locations where Bowery had farms at the time. To complicate the matter, employees in all three locations included some who wanted to follow the rules and some who wanted to defy local regulations. After a lot of back and forth, Bowery decided to require employees at each farm to follow the guidelines in place for their respective state. It took a while to arrive at that conclusion, but it seemed to work for most employees.

Bowery controlled the surroundings of the farm-based employees. Other teams at the company didn't have that protection. The sales team, for instance, had to go into numerous supermarkets on any given day, where they were uncertain of the security protocols in place. In the spring of 2020, it was still unclear how the virus spread. The company listened to the concerns of their sales team and worked with that team to develop solutions that would keep the team safe.

It wasn't clear if the virus could be contracted from the floor in the supermarket aisles. To protect their sales team and their families, Bowery gave the entire sales team a budget so they could buy "work shoes." When the sales team members would get home, they would leave their "work shoes" outside and change into their "home shoes" before going inside. The shoe budget wasn't a huge expense, but it meant a lot to the sales team to be heard, to be taken seriously, and to be treated with kindness. The company needed to understand the sales team's primal and very real concerns for safety and be nimble in its response.

Cooley's attention to her team's psychological safety is in the same spirit as Alison Kear (from Chapter 1) hiring a wellness coach for her team.

If we learned anything during the pandemic, it's that we're never in the same position for long. For Bowery, once the company had the people on the farm comfortable with masks, commuting, and other new elements of their jobs, it was time to require the HQ people to return to the office.

Bowery had opened the office on a voluntary basis fairly early during the pandemic. About half of the corporate staff came in weekly throughout 2020 and 2021. This was a good indicator that being together meant a lot to people. The other half had become accustomed to working from home. Now, Bowery faced the same challenges every other company faced. They needed to bring employees back to the office on terms that met individual employees' needs yet fostered the in-person aspect of company culture that leadership deemed to be so important.

In January 2022, the company announced it would reopen fully in April on Tuesdays through Thursdays. Now it was the corporate team's turn to get stressed. Some balked. Others, particularly those who had been coming in regularly already, were frustrated with those who were pushing back on returning. Much as the company wants to meet employees "where they are," Bowery thinks of itself as an in-person company. Bowery can't change its nature because people don't want to participate in person.

Eight weeks into the new schedule it was apparent that requiring the corporate staff to be in the office three days a week wasn't going to work. It seemed too arbitrary to the employees. Cooley thought they got the solution "mostly right but not absolutely right." The company pivoted again. It decided that any work that could be done independently could be done remotely. Instead of requiring people to be in the office three specific days, the company allowed people to use their judgment to be in the office based on what they needed to get done on any given day. If you needed to brainstorm with others, participate in a decision-making meeting, or interview a candidate, you were expected to be present in person.

That approach has worked well. The company was able to be nimble because it listened to what people wanted and gave them the flexibility they needed. Cooley found that just as important as the decision you make as a leader is the justification behind that decision. "If we didn't get the decision absolutely correct, but we were intentional about our process and conclusion, people gave us the benefit of the doubt as we worked out the kinks."

Cooley shared, "This pivot was really about listening to our people, taking a step back, and thinking about why in-person work mattered. It was then about creating guidance that was rooted in the culture we were building rather than rules that people needed to follow. Once we fully explained the way we wanted to work and why it was important for innovation, speed, and collaboration, everyone was on board."

In this case, being kind to the core manifested itself in listening to the needs of employees. That element of culture at Bowery allowed the company to adjust on the fly and meet the needs of the group.

SUMMARY

Knowing and living your organization's values allows you to stay on track in a crisis. If you are true to those values, articulate them clearly, can justify them, and understand how they impact the organization in calmer times, you're better positioned to adjust as needed in a crisis. You can't "flex" in the moment or adjust course if you don't know your original path and motivations.

TAKEAWAYS

If you have a stated set of values for your organization, assess how you lived those values during Covid or whatever the most recent major challenge has been for your organization. Make that assessment real and tangible for your team. Grade yourself on how you performed in light of each of those values. Then share that assessment publicly. Have your communications team write a column in the next company newsletter about your performance against those goals the way you share any other measurement of success. When you share those results, indicate how following that principle allowed you to remain nimble and respond to the crisis, and how following those values even more closely would have helped further.

If you haven't yet articulated a set of values, now's the time to start. Regardless of the size of your organization, putting words around the group's values requires a lot of conversations and collaboration. Getting the words right takes a lot of listening. You can retain an outside firm to manage the process or have HR tackle the initiative.

Once you have your values defined, talk about them, frequently. Some organizations even include in performance reviews how well staff, especially managers, demonstrate the values. If they are defined clearly and simply, they become accessible. If they are made part of everyday conversations, you can assess how people are applying them.

SUGGESTIONS FOR BRAINSTORMING

To innovate, it helps to foster brainstorming. When facing a new challenge or threat, you need all the ideas you can get. You want to promote an attitude of "How can we do this differently," rather than, "this is how we've always done it." Here are some basic tips on how to encourage creativity and openness when you have to remain nimble.

1. Establish ground rules for the conversation. Nothing kills a meeting faster than when someone criticizes or quashes someone else's ideas. You'll get around to weighing the merits of the ideas later. When you are in the brainstorming phase of a conversation, you want to

promote broader thinking; there are no "bad" ideas at this stage.

If you are leading the discussion, you're responsible for facilitating the open exchange of ideas. When a group member responds to someone else's idea with, "That won't work because of X," you politely but firmly say, "Let's hold off on commenting on the quality of everyone's ideas. Feel comfortable building on other people's ideas, but don't evaluate the ideas yet. We'll have time for that later." If that same person denigrates another idea, use more forceful language, such as, "Again, it won't be helpful to us in reaching our goal if we knock others' ideas. At this stage we're just generating as many ideas as possible."

2. Assign someone to take notes, ideally in a public way such as on a flip chart, or, if you are meeting virtually, on an electronic blackboard so everyone can see the ideas. If you are the leader, encourage the scribe to write down what is being said verbatim. If the scribe wants to tweak the language, they should add their own version. It's demoralizing to meeting participants if every time they offer a suggestion, the note-taker changes their language.

3. After you create the longest list of ideas possible, group together like elements. Make sure as you lead this discussion, you check in with team members that you understood their suggestions correctly.

Evaluating the ideas comes later. At this stage, you just want to promote creativity.

Questions for you and your team to consider:

How does our organization promote that sense of engagement by team members beyond meeting their daily job requirements?

How do we encourage our team members to pitch in?

How did that play out during the pandemic? Were there lasting changes to how we defined roles or assigned tasks?

How well does our organization promote creativity and foster innovation? What concrete steps could we take to foster that attitude?

Are most decisions in meetings handed down from the top branches, or drawn up through the roots of the organization through brainstorming?

Bowery was able to be flexible in the moment, in part, because it saw the problem coming two weeks out. When did our organization begin taking the pandemic seriously? Who or which group at the organization first flagged the issue? What could we have done to heed warnings sooner? Would it have helped?

How does taking care of our colleagues' mental health and sense of personal safety manifest itself during times of upheaval? What added steps did we take, or could we still take, to meet people where they are?

CHAPTER 3

Accept Your Limits

God, grant me the strength to change the things I can, the serenity to accept the things I cannot, and the wisdom to know the difference.
—*The Serenity Prayer*

In times of uncertainty, we look for wisdom anywhere we can find it. When we're faced with significant changes, we sometimes resist the change, and sometimes placate that change hoping things will soon return to "normal." Wisdom helps us know when a subtle tilting is about to accelerate and turn things upside down. It prods us to get on board with adapting.

Accepting that the world is now different and that we're never going back to the way things were gives us the courage to make the changes needed. That allows us to stay relevant and survive. We made the same adjustment after 9/11 and again after the January 6 attack on the Capitol.

In 2020, change hit healthcare like no other industry. Those healthcare systems that realized quickly which of those changes were permanent were able to be nimble and innovate. We can all learn valuable lessons from how they addressed the needs of their patients, their staff, and their community through the most difficult public health crisis of the last hundred years.

PROFILE: MEMORIAL HEALTH – CENTRAL ILLINOIS (HEALTHCARE)

My vaccination card is up to date and sits by the phone in the kitchen right by the back door. It's part of the comfortable clutter now, along with the car keys, spare change, last week's church bulletin, and the mail that came in for the kids that they'll pick up the next time they stop by. The stuff that collects by our door reflects the timely and the timeless elements in our lives. The pandemic brought a new dimension to our personal backstory.

I've never had a medical document that mattered to me before. Covid brought our healthcare history and our healthcare present into focus like no other event in our collective consciousness. It changed how we think about our country's medical response system, even if only to make us more aware of it. I haven't had to pull out that card in a while. Nevertheless, the fact that for over 18 months we had to prove our health status in order to enjoy the mobility we took for granted changed how many of us think about our health.

Every one of us had interactions with healthcare workers during the pandemic. We or a loved one contracted Covid; we had to have other medical needs addressed; or we needed to get vaccinated. We all became hyperaware of the perils and challenges within our healthcare system. Regardless of the challenges within our own industries and our families, we all knew the pressures on the nurses, doctors, EMTs, home healthcare attendants, hospital staff, and government health officials outweighed what we were experiencing. They faced people with debilitating health needs, and some saw patients die, every day, for months on end. The rest of us did what we could to acknowledge and honor their dedication and sacrifice.

Thousands of healthcare workers in this country remained nimble and creative in addressing the pandemic. If we learn from their experience, we can all respond more effectively during the next crisis.

In the pandemic, an urban hospital in the Northeast had a vastly different experience than a rural clinic in the Southwest. Nevertheless, all shared common burdens and managed through with common graces. The experiences and approaches of Memorial Health (Memorial), a regional healthcare service provider in Springfield, Illinois, provide a glimpse for all of us in what was going on behind the curtain in the emergency room and beyond.

Memorial is a healthcare system with $1.5 billion in annual revenue. It operates six hospitals as well as urgent care facilities, primary care locations, specialty clinics, behavioral health clinics, and other avenues for care. Along with Hospital Sisters Health System (HSHS), Memorial provides services across a wide swath of central Illinois. The United States has 6,000+ hospitals and 400+ health systems. Memorial is right in the middle in terms of size and scope. To respond effectively in both the short term and long term, Memorial had to assess which changes to healthcare brought on by the pandemic would be fleeting, and which would be permanent. Their assessment provides a great lesson in critical thinking.

Memorial is organized under three major umbrellas – the Hospital Group, the Ambulatory Group, which deals with all of the facilities and services provided outside of the hospitals, and a system resources group for centralized business functions like finance, HR, and information services. Jay Roszhart is president of the Ambulatory Group. He manages all of Memorial's operations except the hospitals. Roszhart joined Memorial in 2009, and, over time, served as the Manager of People Operations, Director of Case Management & Clinical Integration, and Vice

President of the Ambulatory Group before becoming president of that group in 2019. That experience in various functions of the organization made him the ideal person to be one of the leads for Memorial's response to the pandemic.

Most of us started hearing news about Covid in January 2020, usually in the form of short sound bites on the evening news about some aggressive flu-like virus running rampant in China. Like most of us, I ignored those warnings as just another bit of the evening news that wasn't going to impact me. Roszhart, like most senior healthcare leaders in the United States, paid attention much more closely and started preparing. Having a plan in place helps you identify where you'll need to be nimble down the road.

HEICS

Over the decades, Memorial, like most healthcare providers in the country, had developed a crisis response plan. The healthcare system in this country has its shortcomings, but government directives, institutional planning, corporate oversight, and risk analysis contribute to making it both effective in crises and resilient over time. In the late 1980s, the Federal Emergency Management Agency (FEMA) adopted the Hospital Emergency Incident Command System (HEICS) and strongly suggested every hospital and healthcare system develop and adopt its own structure. Memorial's HEICS includes many components, such as reassigning specific professionals to key roles outside of the norm for limited periods of time during a crisis. The system creates defined roles with both the authority to make decisions and the flexibility to meet the needs of the situation.

Roszhart grew up in Springfield. After earning a BS in molecular biology at the University of Illinois, Urbana-Champaign, he received a Master's in healthcare administration from St. Louis University. He displays an easy sense of humor, a genuine sense of humility, and, most keenly, a deep commitment to meeting the healthcare needs of his local community.

In his time at Memorial, he helped lead the organization through a handful of incidents where HEICS was triggered. Those included massive snowstorms that threatened the hospital's ability to stay open and widespread community power outages. The nature of those incidents meant the HEICS protocols were never needed for more than 48 hours. While the steps and restructuring envisioned under HEICS worked effectively for an incident of a few days, they needed to be adjusted if they were to be helpful as Covid stretched into months and then years. Nevertheless, HEICS helped Roszhart and his team in the early days and weeks of the pandemic and provided at least the rudimentary elements of a response.

In essence, HEICS helps healthcare enterprises consider two sets of questions in a crisis to minimize the impact on patient care, whether the crisis is a plane crash in your area of service or a flood in the hospital basement.

1. Depending on the nature of a particular critical incident, what roles and responsibilities will need to be filled? What key personnel will need to be reassigned to meet those needs?

2. What's the plan of action? How will that plan be communicated? What outcomes are expected?

If you know your team and the unique challenges and strengths of your organization, answering these questions provides your strategy. You aren't in control of the crisis, but you are in control of the elements of your response.

HEICS promotes a "command and control" approach to crisis management. All info is funneled up to the leader, who then provides directives based on having the vantage point of the big picture. In a crisis, tasks that are not part of the ordinary course of business have to be managed. Staff members need to step in and take on different and distinct roles. Those new roles only work if it's clear who has both the authority to make certain decisions and the responsibility for getting certain steps done.

At Memorial, Roszhart was the Incident Commander for the Ambulatory Division. He and his counterpart managing the response at the hospitals reported to the Incident Commander for the entire enterprise. There were clear lines of reporting on all matters. The 30-member leadership team communicated through in-person "staff huddles" two or three times a day. (This was in the days before we all knew about social distancing.)

MEMORIAL'S FIRST STEPS

During Covid, most organizations put their emphasis on keeping Covid out of their buildings and their communities. Memorial's first order of business was to figure out how to welcome infected patients into their locations.

Someone sick or injured is operating outside of their normal daily experience. They need help reorienting. But that state of dealing with the extraordinary is, in fact, the norm at a healthcare center. On the best of days at a health center, you're prepared for crises. But you're prepared for the crises you're *used to* and have practice responding to – car accidents, severe flu, or pneumonia cases, and depending on your location, frostbite or heatstroke. You aren't *expecting* an Ebola outbreak, a gang turf war, or a chemical explosion at the local plant. You're ready for *your kind* of chaos, not chaos in general.

One of the earliest questions Memorial faced was what to do when a patient arrived at a clinic clearly in distress with a disease we knew little about. It was all the more challenging when that patient was followed by dozens more in the same situation. At Memorial, like elsewhere, they had to create protocols that changed daily based on the latest info from the CDC and other countries' health organizations. The details of the protocols changed based on directives regarding scientific analysis in the United States and from cooperating healthcare systems around the globe. The actual implementation of the protocols changed based on the realities on the ground. The team had to be nimble based on not just each new government directive, but also on the availability of staff, of testing, and of personal protective equipment (PPE), among other factors.

PROTOCOLS AND PARKING LOTS

It's one thing to have to rethink a protocol. It's another to have to rethink the layout of the waiting room, the hospital entrance, and the use of every individual space in the building. At Memorial, employees were constantly adapting. They had to be nimble in the way they dressed, prepared, structured their space, and used their time.

One of the first steps Roszhart and his team took was to fit 300 clinical professionals with masks and portable respirators. This was made more complicated by the ever-changing availability of both items. (These "respirators" are the types of facemasks with a breathing apparatus attached. The "ventilators" we heard so much about during the pandemic were to assist patients who couldn't breathe.) Because of supply shortages, Memorial couldn't get enough of any one respirator, so staff had to use whatever was available.

At one point, healthcare workers were using seven types of respirators, and there were three different methods for performing a "fit test." Each test required selecting the right size respirator for the person based on the size and shape of their face. After the "subject" was fitted, he or she would don a large hood into which a sweet or sour scent would be sprayed. If the subject could smell or taste the scent, the respirator wasn't filtering out the particles and the respirator had to be re-fitted. They also needed a process to track which masks and respirators – and in what size – fit each person.

If someone was fitted for one type but that type wasn't available on a given day, they had to be fitted for another type. Roszhart had to make sure the process was being managed correctly and understand what his staff was dealing with, so he learned how to fit the respirators on his colleagues. The process was cumbersome, and one person could only fit about 10–15 people per day. In February 2020, no one at Memorial had the job title "respirator fitter." By April, through a process of "training the trainers," there were dozens of people who could step in and help as more people needed to be fitted for different gear.

CDC guidelines for hospitals didn't just include PPE usage. Hospitals were also required to disinfect any room in which an "aerosol generating procedure" took place. Unfortunately, even a simple nose swab is considered an aerosol-generating procedure by the CDC. Disinfecting a room takes between 30 and 60 minutes – a huge time commitment for the facilities' staff, and an enormous impact on efficiency for any hospital already strapped for space. It's especially burdensome if you have 400 people waiting in line outside to be tested.

Memorial couldn't control the rules being handed down, but it could control how it used its space and whose help it could request. Like many hospitals, Memorial coped by setting up tents in its parking lots. With an open-air environment, the need to disinfect the "room" was diminished. Roszhart became an expert in how to set up tents and build drive-through facilities, something his degree in molecular biology hadn't prepped him for.

As testing quickly became available, the hospital needed to figure out how to have a drive-through testing area that would accommodate 300–400 cars in a parking lot that holds only 30.

Being nimble now required Memorial's leadership team to:

- rethink its space to meet new demands,

- rework its relationships with neighbors whose businesses would be impacted by traffic jams, and

- renegotiate with local authorities whose help would be needed to help manage the flow of cars.

All of this re-working of their service delivery model required brainpower and creativity. To add complexity, it was all happening when teams were shorthanded because staff was getting sick and quarantine rules mandated some people stay home even if they were not infected. On a *good* day, the entire world is shorthanded when it comes to people who are creative and good at solving problems. If you now sideline a sizable part of the population, you're further handicapped.

Roszhart sounds like a military leader headed into battle when he says, "I had to redeploy people." Sometimes this meant staff did its line function but in a different location. For instance, as more people got sick, urgent care nurse practitioners became ICU nurses. Other times, that assignment meant just getting someone – anyone – to get certain tasks completed. Using a standard triage method, he figured out what jobs needed to get done now and which could wait. He needed frontline workers.

Memorial's HEICS restructuring plans included a new role of "Section Chief" in charge of re-deployment. That person needed to determine who had the skill set to step into each new role that was needed. If ever there was a role that needed to be nimble, it would be the "Section Chief in Charge of Re-Deployment." "Our billers, coders, and leaders at all levels were trained on how to take swab tests – quite outside their comfort zone," Roszhart said. Primary care doctors and nurse practitioners were assigned to similar roles. Your title, rank, and ego were irrelevant; you were needed on the front lines. Those individuals needed to be nimble both in learning a new skill not exactly on their bucket list and in adapting an attitude of openness to contributing in any way that was needed.

Attitude was crucial at this point in the crisis. The rank-and-file staff was asked to be creative and flexible on a daily basis. Workers needed to see senior leaders acting with the same kind of agility. A positive, can-do attitude by leaders would be crucial for the process to succeed. Again, one element you can control when you respond to a crisis is how you show up as a leader.

THE EVOLUTION OF DECISION-MAKING

The HEICS plan was intended for short-duration changes to a hospital's reporting structure and org chart. Extending that plan for 18 months revealed the cracks in the system. The hospital team had to revisit the plan repeatedly, which became the norm in so many ways during the pandemic. The "command and control" system had to evolve into a more collaborative decision-making structure.

According to Roszhart, people tend to overreact in the short term and underreact in the long term. You miss opportunities to remake your business if you keep thinking that everything will "return to normal." You have to figure out and accept what elements of your business model have changed for good instead of resisting that change. You don't have to be happy about the changes, but you can't pretend they aren't happening. You have to embrace the evolution. Roszhart suggests that Covid completely changed the core business model of healthcare. Healthcare systems like Memorial have to be nimble enough to react to the long-term implications of their situation.

One of the biggest challenges for any entity in a crisis is making decisions that are the right move in the short term, but will undoubtedly have negative impacts in the long term. For Memorial, it was the right move at the time to close some primary care facilities such as doctors' offices. All of the PPE that would have gone to those locations was needed at the clinics and hospitals. But closing those facilities deprived patients of access to services for ongoing, chronic health conditions such as diabetes. As a result, patients who would normally have sought care sooner at a doctor's office would wait until their situation became acute and would end up in urgent care facilities.

It's when all of your options are bad that you need more brainpower. The "command and control" model of decision-making works well when you want quick decisions. Its effectiveness is limited when you need to make the tougher calls that will have lasting impact. That's when you need a more inclusive and collaborative decision-making process. Some on the Memorial leadership team might have remained stuck in a response plan that was no longer working. Recognizing that Memorial had control over how it stuck to or adapted its plan allowed Memorial to be more nimble.

COMMUNICATION

We all know that communication during a crisis is crucial. But "communicating" means more than sending out information. It means focusing on where we're gathering information.

In Chapter 1, you read how the team at Covenant House networked on so many levels to gather good ideas, avoid the mistakes others had encountered, and develop creative solutions.[1] Another of the five drivers of innovation beyond networking involves observing the people and processes around us. Our capacity to innovate is limited by our own level of creativity. Our creativity expands as we expose ourselves to more – and more diverse – ideas.

Reading reports and updates on what's happening in your organization helps you gather data, but it doesn't give you the feel for the lived experience of others. We should think about who we should listen to and gather the perspectives of those closest to the lines of conflict. We can gather that information not just from reading and listening, but also from observing others in action; that's where we uncover the pain points.

You can gather that information by getting out and seeing how things in your organization are working in the field. "In times of crisis," according to Roszhart, "you can't lead from behind a desk."

On a tour through one of his clinics, Roszhart listened in as a staff member called a patient to let her know her Covid test result came back positive. The staff member walked the patient through the quarantine protocols and then listened as the patient asked about how she could adjust the protocols so that she could continue to care for her elderly parents. The call took about 10 minutes. When Roszhart asked the staff member about the call and how she was doing, she said, "I want to take a moment after each call and think about how to help this person, but I have literally 300 calls to make today, and I don't know how I'm going to get all of this done. These people are waiting for their results." Roszhart knew they needed to find another way to streamline this process. He wouldn't have appreciated the complexity of the situation or the emotional impact on his team members if his analysis had been based on a spreadsheet. He was able to re-direct resources and create processes to help his team members manage their time and accomplish their goals.

You will, however, frequently send out key messages. The method of communication is important since you need to get people what they need unencumbered with the clutter. Memorial relied heavily on texting and Workplace by Facebook. In a crisis, we all tend to have a short attention span as we are juggling information coming in from lots of directions. Roszhart found that short and simple messages tended to be most helpful for most communication in those situations.

COMING TO CONCLUSIONS

At Memorial, as the months wore on, they realized that they would have to evolve their thinking. They needed to move from "This is how we'll do it for now," to, "How do we implement a new approach for the long haul and still get our jobs done?" Roszhart says, "We called it our 'New Normal' planning." For developing longer-term strategic planning, they needed to find better guidance than the "command and control" approach provided. The answer, though, was right in front of them. They had the brain power they needed; they just had to harvest it differently.

"We had the 'Covid Cave,'" Roszhart recalls. "When we met, we would listen to each other, argue pros and cons. We all, at different points, had to live with trade-offs. But when we came out of those meetings, we were all on board with the decisions." Roszhart's team in the Covid Cave brought a world of expertise to the conversation. He relied on team members' input, trusted their judgment, and counted on their execution.

This pivot from command and control to a collaborative discussion helped the team remain nimble. One innovation they made to meet one short-term challenge evolved into a permanent solution to a different problem. As noted earlier, as early as mid-March 2020, Memorial started testing people for Covid in the parking lot of one of its clinics. The main purpose was to diminish the stress on hospital emergency rooms and doctors' offices so they could care for other patients. Initially, patients were pulling up in their cars in the parking lot and getting nasal swab testing by a clinic staff member (or a billing clerk retrained for that purpose).

To deal with weather conditions, Memorial built tents to ease the burden on both staff and patients as infection rates spiked and ebbed over the months, Roszhart realized how essential the outdoor testing facilities had become.

In December 2021, the hospital was screening over 1,000 patients per week at the drive-through facilities. That would have created an enormous burden on an ER. The process worked well and created efficiencies for everyone. As a result, Memorial built two custom-designed drive-through testing facilities, each with three bays, which allowed lab technicians to perform respiratory tests, take blood samples, and perform other routine tests more efficiently. Memorial even has "chatbots" deliver test results and create doctors' notes that are sent to the patient's school or employer. This type of "person in the loop" technology is all managed through secure platforms that are compliant with the Health Insurance Portability and Accountability Act (HIPAA).

Not every decision was perfect, but every decision was made with patient and staff safety in mind. "The screwups are OK as long as you learn from them and use them to drive better decisions," Roszhart noted.

"LONG COVID"

Some Covid patients experienced lingering effects of the disease for months after their initial infections: persistent coughs, aches that wouldn't subside, an ongoing loss of smell and taste long after the fevers had subsided. Similarly, our hospitals, clinics, and healthcare workers have experienced longer periods of trauma.

Trauma to the System

For most healthcare systems, elective procedures bring in the income that pays for all of the critical care that takes place. Early in the pandemic, Memorial, like most hospitals, shut down everything elective for three to four months. That eliminated 50% of its income. The hospital was on track to experience a loss of $100 million on a $1.3 billion budget. Before it was clear the government was going to step in and support hospitals with additional Medicaid advancements, FEMA support, or other government payments, Memorial was forced to lay off about 10% of its nonclinical staff. No commercial enterprise wants to go through a layoff. Layoffs are especially difficult at a time when you desperately need your team.

As government programs to support hospitals provided funds, Memorial had to be nimble in how it rehired staff, thinking through the right roles to bring back online, the right way to resource talent, and the best way to reinvigorate stalled initiatives.

In 2021, government payments to help with increased Covid costs helped Memorial end the year $100 million in the black. It ended the next fiscal year on September 30, 2022, with a $225 million deficit on a $1.4 billion budget. That kind of whipsaw in finances makes planning difficult.

The current challenges for Memorial and other healthcare providers will require a continued ability to think creatively and nimbly.

Working in healthcare is less attractive to many younger people. As a result, healthcare systems will need to pay more for full-time employees. In the meantime, they will need to rely more heavily on higher-paid contract workers. According to Roszhart, retaining nursing staff on a contract basis costs healthcare systems, on average, four times what it would cost to have that same level of resources available on a permanent basis. Half of the $225 million deficit for their last fiscal year previously noted is composed of paying for nursing care on a contract basis.

The current year-over-year outlook on income and EBITA (earnings before interest, taxes, and amortization) suggests that Memorial, like many health systems and hospitals, could be in violation of its public bond covenants. That will impact its rating with financial rating agencies, which will impact its interest rates, and increase its debt. The staff costs will continue to increase. Memorial just added 25% to its budget for clinical teams. These are huge challenges.

Memorial, and many healthcare systems, need to turn around their operations. Roszhart says he would hire 300–400 more nurses immediately if he could find them. But to truly meet the level of care needed in the area it serves, the hospital would need an additional 600 nurses. Given the demand and the economy at the moment, whatever resources Memorial finds will be at a premium, somewhere between the current salary levels and the contractor rates it has had to pay during Covid. It's the only way the hospital can compete for talent.

Trauma to the Staff

During Covid, we were all reacting to outside stimuli, such as directives from the government or our employers. Those shifts in our behavior happened quickly and reflexively, in part, because we had no choice. The sign on the supermarket door says, "Masks Required" so we put on a mask because we need bread and milk. The shift in our attitude doesn't happen quite so quickly and involves a lot more baggage. While we all put on our mask going into the store, some of us did so begrudgingly, and some did so eager to be part of the solution.

According to Roszhart, early in the pandemic, the local Springfield community was overwhelmingly supportive of its healthcare workers. On multiple occasions when he was directing traffic in the clinics' parking lot, people drove up just to hand him a cup of coffee or bring lunch to the workers in the tents. But as the pandemic wore on, the mood changed. People became angry as they received a positive test result, and didn't appreciate when a doctor, or, more likely, a nurse, told them they would need to isolate and inform family and friends they had tested positive.

Incidents of violence against healthcare workers continued to rise throughout 2022.[2] According to Roszhart, the second half of 2022 saw more crimes of violence against nurses and frontline healthcare workers than ever before, not just in Illinois, but nationwide. While the vast majority of patients continue to act civilly and take their diagnoses in stride, others lash out.

At Memorial, in the fall of 2022, one patient, upon receiving a positive Covid diagnosis, punched the nurse practitioner who gave him the news. Another trashed the waiting room upon hearing he needed to quarantine. Memorial's response to acts of violence evolved during the pandemic. Early on, the organization was patient when people expressed frustration, and appreciated the volatility and confusion of the situation for all those involved. But healthcare workers have a difficult enough job without becoming the literal punching bag for other people's lack of coping skills. To protect its staff and provide a safe working environment, Memorial now works with law enforcement to prosecute anyone who threatens or attacks its employees.

SUMMARY

We all had to deal with challenges to both our physical space and our inner psyche during Covid. But most of us weren't facing decisions in the pressure-cooker environment that those in the healthcare industry faced. Having a strategic plan for dealing with a crisis and acknowledging when change is happening beyond our control allow us to adapt our plan in the moment to meet the circumstances. If you continue to gather information from various sources, remain open to altering your plan as needed, regardless of how well designed it might be, and show up with the right attitude, you give your team the confidence they need to think and act more nimbly.

If you are pragmatic and honest about what is within your control and what isn't, you can prioritize effectively.

TAKEAWAYS

Some industries are mandated to have a disaster recovery plan. Small companies have plans in place for recovering their data but are unlikely to have a plan ready for reconfiguring the entire workflow of the organization. If you want to be more nimble in response to future crises, consider the following aspects of your business.

1. What aspects of our organization do I control?

    (a) What percent of my employees are full-time versus contract workers? How does that impact my ability to both scale up or down based on need, but also ensure that I have the committed workforce I'll need in the moment?

    (b) How flexible is my office space? What's a "need to have," a "nice to have," and a "definitely can do without"?

    (c) Is our workforce sufficiently connected to our IT network to allow for the greatest flexibility?

2. How agile is my team emotionally and intellectually? Will we realize and own when the situation changes, and we need to shift our plans? How open will the team be to letting go of long-held perspectives and realize that the paradigm for our business has shifted permanently? If my team is slow-moving, what kind of practice or training would help it build a more fluid approach to solving problems?

3. When confronted with change, assess what elements of the change are positive. Acknowledging the helpful elements of the change helps you remain open. Remaining open helps you to develop more concrete strategies to move forward.

Questions for you and your team to consider:

1. What rules from the local, state, and federal governments within which we work required more nimbleness from us? What are the practical and physical realities of our work that made it harder to implement government mandates?

2. How visible were our leaders to those on the front lines?

3. What was our version of "fitting people for masks," the technical adaptation we needed to make on a very personal level that is unique to our industry or company? How well did those processes work, and what could we have done to improve them?

4. What decisions did we have to make during Covid that were based on the choice between two detrimental options? When all of our options are unfavorable, how do we weigh the outcomes and determine our path forward?

5. What questions were we able to ask our group, and what voices did we pull into the conversation that allowed us to make better decisions?

6. What information did we gather by walking around and seeing our team in action?

7. What policies or procedures did we put in place during Covid that became our new standard operating procedure? What new structures or approaches could we still make permanent?

8. What clear missteps can we identify and what did we learn from those mistakes?

PART II

ASK THE RIGHT QUESTIONS

Jack be nimble. Jane be quick. The least of your
problems is the candlestick.

In business, we take calculated risks all the time. We make our
decisions in the context of known parameters, an understanding of our environment, and a feel for the likely reactions of our
colleagues, clients, and other stakeholders. When we jump the
proverbial candlestick, we've factored in the height of the candle, the intensity of the flame, and our self-perception of our
ability to gain air. But what happens when our certainty in those
parameters fails? How do we continue to make decisions when
the rules change, the environment is unknown, and the reactions
of those around us become unpredictable?

We'll be better prepared if we have higher quality information. We'll gather that information if we ask better questions
and inquire of the right sources. In this section, the people and
organizations you'll meet share insights on how they approach

gathering information at times of transition. We'll see that staying open to new information means remaining humble, being willing to challenge even your most basic assumptions about yourself and your organization, and then staying abreast of the information that impacts your industry. All three elements are important if we are going to remain productive and effective in this new age of change.

CHAPTER 4

Think Beyond Yourself

> When we are humble, we have nothing to fear, nothing to lose. We easily flow with the circumstances that we find ourselves in and are endlessly open to learn, to practice, and to transform ourselves.
>
> *—Thich Nhat Hanh – Buddhist Monk*

What could be more relevant to being nimble than the idea of flowing easily with the circumstances around us? When we swim upstream, we're not nimble; we're exhausted. We're nimble when we figure out how to use the current in which we find ourselves to either move faster downstream or get to shore. But allowing the current to take us means abandoning our effort to control our direction. Letting go requires both a great deal of humility and a great deal of trust.

In a rapidly changing business world, we don't control the stream; we control our response to it. We don't control what information is available; we control what information we deem relevant. We don't control who is available for advice; we control how wide we cast the net for that advice.

The pandemic saw tremendous fluidity in the workforce. Many lost their jobs. Those who kept their jobs were connected to their co-workers differently. In addition to dealing with changes inflicted upon us, we sometimes create our own personal disruptions. In 2021 and 2022, a record number of employees chose to change employers ... or careers ... or countries. "The Great Resignation," sometimes also called "The Great Reshuffle," saw many people trying to rethink and re-evaluate the "gain" in "gainful employment."

When we leave one employer, or role, or industry for another, we're in learning mode. Our senses are heightened. To gain confidence and proficiency, we need to practice new skill sets and be conscious of our new surrounds. We can't be on autopilot. Finally, by learning and practicing, we transform ourselves, as Nhat Hanh says.

If we are leading a team, we're not just working on these skills for ourselves. We're providing the space and support for others to do the same. Whether we are adapting to our own new circumstances or helping new teammates adapt to theirs, we have to remain nimble, remain humble, and trust in those around us.

PROFILE – TECHNOLOGY – MAKING TRANSITIONS – LEARN, PRACTICE, AND TRANSFORM

The early 2020s saw a tremendous spike in the number of people changing jobs. The "Great Reshuffling" occurred at all levels in organizations and for a wide array of reasons. In Q3 2022, Matt van Geldere moved from a role as Chief Transformation Officer at a global adtech company to become the Chief People Officer of a fintech company. In both roles, he has had to manage not just his own professional growth but that of hundreds of his companies' employees.

As Chief Transformation Officer at his prior employer, a global adtech company, van Geldere had been leading a merger and acquisition (M&A) integration project for an acquisition target based in Russia. After more than a year of strategizing and negotiating, the parties reached agreement. The transaction was set to close in Q1 2022. Just days before the close, Russia invaded Ukraine. The deal was suspended indefinitely. This left van Geldere in a bit of limbo. His role was tied to executing the deal and then managing the transitions that would follow. With the deal now unlikely to happen, he realized the time was right to find a new challenge.

While he considered a number of options, most would require him moving from his base in Singapore, something he wasn't interested in doing. Then, a head hunter introduced him to Thunes, a cross-border payment business.

Van Geldere's background was in adtech, the technology behind marketing toward specific audiences and measuring the success of advertising campaigns. He had no background in fintech, the technology behind financial services transactions. However, as someone with decades of experience in human resources, he had helped countless people transition from one role to another. He knew that success in any given role usually requires two things:

1. proficiency at the skills needed to do the job, and

2. familiarity with the context in which the skills are being used.

While both factors play a role in someone's success, they require different learning curves. Knowing if you are right for a new role involves assessing whether you can both develop the new skill set and adapt to the new setting.

Thunes, only a few years old, already had 450 people around the globe, and was poised to continue growing quickly. Van Geldere was confident he could help the company expand its team and grow its talent. He knew how to help companies transform, the skill set needed at Thunes at that moment. His experience in adtech provided him the road map for helping his new colleagues succeed.

Van Geldere's approach to his employers, his colleagues, his roles, the fast-moving worlds of adtech and fintech, and the faster-moving world of emerging markets, centers on remaining nimble, finding ways to add value, and asking the right questions. He had to be nimble himself in learning a new industry. Although fintech and adtech are both tech-focused, they involve different players, different regulations, and different vibes. To van Geldere, being nimble is about accepting that you need to start again to learn about a business. It means accepting that you don't know a lot and being willing to listen, *that is*, to learn.

Learning Requires Humility

When the Covid pandemic hit, Thunes was in its infancy, with a small number of employees. Many companies are now trying to return to a pre-pandemic normalcy. Thunes never had one for the vast majority of staff. Ninety percent of its employees, including van Geldere, joined the company since the start of 2020 and had no experience of reporting to work at a Thunes office. As the head of employee engagement, van Geldere is less worried about hiring people than he is about retaining people, especially in a world where people seem to change jobs with increasing frequency.

His thoughts about remote work echo what I heard from clients throughout the pandemic. Among other tragedies, Covid sucked all the fun part of work out of the experience, leaving us with only the "work" part of work. "With an entirely remote workforce, work becomes very transactional," van Geldere says. "If all of our interactions at work are transactional, we're all just independent contractors instead of a team. We have to work a lot harder at building relationships. You have to work harder at building trust." The transactional approach to our work relationships certainly contributed to the "Great Reshuffling."

One young employee shared with him that he had been at a few companies in just the last few years. When he would switch roles, he said, he would log off of one group Zoom meeting on a Friday afternoon, and log onto a new group on Monday morning. The faces and the backgrounds in the little windows would change, but not much else. "If that's an employee's experience with your company, that's deadly from a corporate culture perspective," van Geldere warns.

And the needs of the team evolve, which is where being nimble comes in. According to van Geldere, one of the biggest learning curves he's experienced in the last few years is around the role that humility plays in a successful organization. If leaders think they have all the answers, they stop listening to those around them.

Van Geldere led the cross-functional team that managed the Covid response at his prior company. Although it was a challenging experience on many levels, he and others on the team found it to be an almost refreshing experience. "There was no jockeying for position on the committee. No one was vying to be the Chief Pandemic Response Officer at the end of the process," he said. As a result, all of the politics fell by the wayside and people just cooperated and got the job done. As President Harry Truman once said, "It's amazing what you can accomplish when you don't care who gets the credit."

During that time van Geldere saw management responding with humility with regard to both the pandemic and the Russian invasion of Ukraine. Both were unexpected, and no one in leadership had dealt with the issues before, so no one pretended to have experience managing these situations. No board of directors would hold its CEO accountable for not having had a pandemic response plan in place. No one in leadership now was in a leadership role the last time one Eastern European country invaded another.

As a result, senior leaders turned to their teams and spent more time asking questions than giving direction. In watching senior leaders at his previous company handle both the Russian invasion and pandemic, van Geldere was impressed with how well they listened. "They approved the plans of the designated teams without playing the 'we-know-better' card," he says.

Practice (i.e., Repetition) Builds Trust

The humility that prompts us to listen well also prods us to adopt that behavior consistently. While we might suddenly feel trust for someone after witnessing a single instance of their behavior, we only maintain that level of trust if we see that person behaving similarly on a routine basis. Trust is complicated, and it's essential to getting people on board with our ideas and willing to follow us in times of turmoil.

In *The Power of Trust: How Companies Built It, Lose It, Regain It*,[1] Sandra Sucher and Shalene Gupta define a trusting relationship.

> *When we choose to trust someone, we willingly give them power over us, trusting that they will not abuse this power. Trust is a special form of dependence, and is predicated on the idea that we can be more than disappointed; we can be betrayed.*[2]

When we are maneuvering in unknown waters, we feel vulnerable. We grab on to anything that feels solid and safe. A leader who has shown consistency becomes the rock of stability we need. That leader has given us confidence that we won't be betrayed.

There were two actions by van Geldere and the senior leaders at the adtech company during the management of the pandemic that led the employees to trust them. First, they not only listened, they also asked the types of questions that showed they actually cared, and they asked those questions frequently enough to respond as the situation changed. Second, they admitted when they got things wrong. Van Geldere is now applying that same approach at Thunes.

Asking the Right Questions at the Right Time and for the Right Reason

Regularly checking in with your team and asking questions is essential. It's not about constant employee surveys. It's about asking individuals what they need in the moment. Calling colleagues settling into a remote work environment asking,

"What do you need?" might result in them getting the stand-up desk or the Wi-Fi signal booster they need to be more productive. In addition, it might provide you with the good-will you need from them to get better commitment to your shared cause.

Questions that encourage genuine responses rather than seek agreement promote trust because they influence how people view our motives. If I ask you, "How can I help?" I'm giving you the opportunity to guide the conversation and determine parameters. By asking you what's important to you rather than assuming I know what's important, I convey genuine interest in meeting your needs. My purpose in asking defines what I want to achieve, in this case, helping you have what you need to do your job. The reason I want to achieve that goal defines my motive. If I'm perceived as wanting to help you in order to make your work life easier, you presume a positive motive behind my actions and are more likely to trust me.[3]

By contrast, if my questions begin with, "Don't you think that…?" I'm not looking to learn about your needs. I'm looking to get you to agree with me. If I'm helping you do your job more effectively purely for my own benefit of achieving more output from you, my motive is suspect, and I've undermined trust. The presumed motive behind my question is what promotes or undermines your trust in me.[4]

Aristotle defined the penchant for acting in "the right manner" as "moral virtue," and argued that our natural tendency as humans is to seek out others who not only behave properly toward us but do so for the right reasons. He also argued that we learn this behavior through habit rather than by reason.[5] That means we can build trust with others if we develop the habits of acting with clear, less-selfish motives. If we have the trust of those around us, we're more likely to get their buy-in when we need to leverage their ideas, change course, and move quickly, that is, be nimble.

At Thunes, van Geldere has hired "workplace experience managers," whose job is to create office environments that are attractive to people. "They're not there to turn on the coffee machine or manage the AC," he says. "We need to think creatively about how to make coming into the office *valuable* for people. We need to make sure people feel the benefit of collaborating with others in person, and to help them experience the 'fun' part of work; the camaraderie that's built when you do things together and in person." The workplace experience managers are implementing the ideas that employees have already shared with senior leaders. But a big part of their role is simply to keep asking questions and listening.

Acknowledging Mistakes

Admitting you don't have all the answers helps you get the job done because it prompts you to go to others for their substance or advice. Admitting when you make a mistake becomes crucial to building trust.

Van Geldere shares, "On more than one occasion during the handling of the pandemic at my previous company, I sent messages saying, 'We got this wrong, and now we're going to do it a different way.' We got a lot of credit from employees for admitting our errors and gained a lot of credibility." Van Geldere's note to employees conveyed that he knew the company was still learning. They were taking in the feedback from employees (i.e., listening) and growing from that knowledge.

TRANSFORMING REQUIRES ACCEPTANCE – "TRUST" AS A TWO-WAY STREET

In the age of the "Great Reshuffling," the vulnerability that goes along with trust puts tremendous power in the hands of valuable employees. As an advisor to many law firm and consulting firm clients, I've heard repeatedly in the last few years that firms hesitate before giving associates any constructive feedback out of concern the person might become upset and leave. A reluctance to provide feedback creates a significant challenge if your role is to help someone grow their skills set.

At his prior employer, where van Geldere led the Covid response team, the culture had always emphasized the importance of being in the office. Working from home had been frowned on. As a result, the company hadn't put the infrastructure in place for people to work remotely when the pandemic hit. But the bigger challenge wasn't around how to get people laptops. It was shifting the mindset of managers who felt they couldn't "manage" someone who wasn't sitting next to them.

Proximity bias is the concept that people in positions of power tend to treat workers who are physically closer to them more favorably. It correlates with the "halo effect," a centuries-old concept that if we like and value one attribute of someone, we are likely to ascribe other positive attributes toward them. If we are physically in the office more, our colleagues who are also present in person have a more positive view of us because of proximity bias, which, in turn, provides us with a halo effect, giving us even more clout – a double benefit. If we don't come into the office, whether by choice or circumstances, we have to find other ways to build our credibility and our relationships.

In van Geldere's experience, the managers at his former employer felt more confident of the work ethic of the people who were physically closest to them even if they couldn't demonstrate that the person in the office was, in fact, more productive than a peer working from home. Those managers felt they could observe those colleagues in real time and interact with them as needed. That left them with a halo effect toward those employees, which was suspended during lockdown but is now resurgent in a hybrid work environment.

Thunes continues to expand into more regions and interact with players in diverse cultures. "Senior leaders can't sit in Singapore or London and pretend they know in detail what's going on locally in our remote markets. They need to build local teams and trust those teams," van Geldere notes. He believes that global companies can't rely on sending "home office" leaders to live the expatriate (expat) life in another location as a long-term solution. It's not only parochial in thinking, it's just not feasible. While the pandemic may be declared over, the psychological effects will linger for years. Singapore alone has lost hundreds of thousands of expat workers across all levels in the last few years. While some will return, many will not.

Thunes is aggressively growing its local talent, not just in Singapore, but in Nairobi, Beijing, Barcelona, and other key locations. By growing local talent, Thunes is conveying its commitment to those regions and behaving consistently with its promises, which goes a long way toward building trust.

In times of crisis, employees routinely ask themselves, "Can I trust my leaders?" In periods like the "Great Reshuffling," leadership has to grapple with the fundamental question: "Do we trust our employees?" Coming back to the time of the pandemic, in addition to seasoned professionals, van Geldere's previous employer had hundreds of people in hubs in Barcelona and Boston – typically in their mid- to late-twenties. Those employees were mostly far from home and in their first or second job after university. They had hoped to live the mythical "young professional" life of freedom and excitement while launching their careers. During the pandemic, the company leaders were concerned that these new hires were going to sit at home gaming all day or watching the baby or walking the dog rather than working.

A new CEO had joined the adtech firm only six months prior to Covid. Her work experience had been mostly in the United States. Most of the team sat in Europe. She decided they had to operate from a place of trust. It was a pivotal moment for the company. Team members figured out how to get laptops to each person. They on-boarded 100 new starters without bringing them to the office. They gave them ongoing coaching and attention to help them feel connected. The effort took a nimble approach and a nimble mindset, but it worked.

Deeper Reflection

Having humility as a leader isn't just about asking questions about others. It's also about asking questions of ourselves.

Our brain doesn't just help us think; it helps us justify why we act the way we just did or are about to. Our brain tells us we are good people who act with justice and benevolence, even when we aren't and don't.[6]

Many of us find ourselves in leadership roles because we have had more experience than others and have made better judgment calls. Believing we are rightfully in our roles gives us confidence in our decisions, which allows us to make decisions quickly and respond to situations nimbly. That's essential for helping us move our organization forward. That means that although we gather input from many sources, our experience and judgment help us decide how to weigh that input to reach a conclusion that achieves the greater good.

But it doesn't mean our decisions are always calculated objectively. If we want to be more nimble, and think and act more quickly, we have to challenge our own motives. Motive not only contributes toward how well we build trust with others, it also has a significant impact on the quality of our decisions. When making decisions in times of change, when quick responses are needed and there is limited time to think through the issues, here are three questions you can ask yourself to buffer against making your decisions based on suspect motives.

1. To what extent is my ego influencing my decision? In other words, am I pushing a certain course of action because it was my idea versus it's the best idea that has been put forth? Am I advocating a position because it makes me look good versus because it's the right decision?

2. To what extent is my own self-interest influencing this decision? This is different from how my ego is impacted. Ego is often public, influenced on how others view us. Self-interest may be hidden from others. Those around us may not know how we might benefit from a particular course of action. But we do. Are we letting our selfishness impact our decisions?

3. To what extent am I part of the problem? This is a tough one. It takes a tremendous willingness to be self-critical to determine objectively whether we are helping or hurting in a particular situation. Separating our *intent* – or our self-perception of our intent – from our *impact* requires an honest assessment of this issue.

Adding these questions to whatever decision-making matrix we each use will help us make better decisions and remain more nimble. Building the habit of asking these questions will help us build the moral virtue Aristotle advocated to help others to trust us.

Takeaways

To act more nimbly and make better decisions in the moment, we usually need better data, better understanding of the people around us, and better self-awareness so that we don't get in our own way. This means:

- including others in our discussions,
- doing so genuinely and consistently, and
- internalizing the needs of others to motivate them from a more genuine place.

In other words, we need to learn, to practice, and to transform.

As Aristotle indicated, adopting better behaviors doesn't start with adopting a mindset; it starts with adopting habits. Here are three questions you can practice asking that will transform you into a good listener:

1. How can I help?
2. What would be most helpful to you?
3. Would it be helpful to you if I _____?

As you adopt the habit of asking these questions, you will become a better listener. As you achieve a reputation for being a good listener, you will build more trust with those around you.

When you ask these questions, you prompt yourself to remain open and challenge your own assumptions. You transform yourself. (Nhat Hanh would be proud.)

How can you then keep your ego in check as you make decisions? It would be a bit awkward to have a card on your desk that says, "How much am I part of the problem?" but who knows. It might help.

Alternatively, you could work with your group on creating an environment that promotes an open spirit of debate. One client I work with has adopted a motto of "assuming positive intent." Its corporate Code of Conduct specifies that when employees ask questions about a manager's decision, the manager must assume the employee is asking the question out of genuine concern and a desire to understand rather than based on some nefarious motive. That approach has helped the company build better psychological safety for all employees and a healthier work environment with better, more robust conversations and decision-making.

What would be the impact of that type of motto at your organization?

Questions for you and your team to consider:

1. How does our culture welcome input from across the spectrum of employees and other stakeholders?

2. When I hear someone else's ideas, do I automatically judge, or do I ask questions first to understand their perspective and vantage point?

(continued)

(continued)

3. Are the questions I ask truly framed so that I learn rather than reinforce my pre-conceived notions?

4. Once I've asked questions, what steps can I take to verify the information learned?

5. What effort do we put forth to build trust across the organization?

CHAPTER 5

Learn What Others Value

If you want to go fast, go alone. If you want to go far,
go together.

—African Proverb

If we want to go fast *and* go far, we need to bring our team with us. Dragging people with us kicking and screaming does not create a "nimble" group. We are more likely to succeed if we inspire people to hone their innovative instincts, and help them develop both an inquisitive mindset and creative and collaborative behaviors. We can't control when massive change will impact the economy, our industry, or our own organization. We can, however, build our team in a way that allows us to respond when we need to be nimble. To do so requires asking ourselves what kind of team we need in place to be more successful, both at recruiting talent and building that talent to serve our clients.

Teams come in many shapes and sizes. A unit of military recruits forges into a team during training. A gaggle of grade-school soccer players learns to act as a team as they respond to the often-exasperated calls from the coach on the sideline. Your tech/sales/associate/analyst cohort joined your organization as individuals, and some may still function as independent contributors. But if you want to go fast and go far in the nimble-necessary environment we all live in now, you'll need to consolidate that cohort into a cohesive, collaborative pack of professionals. First, you should consider what kind of team you need to succeed. Second, you should develop that team's instincts and skills. In this chapter, we'll look at how one organization advises its clients to do both.

Profile: PwC (Consulting) Encouraging Trust as a Bonding Agent

As we saw in Part I, to increase your flexibility and your nimbleness in times of upheaval, it can be helpful to keep your organization's mission and values in mind as your guiding star. That becomes especially true, particularly complicated, and uniquely urgent if your firm's mission is simply "To build trust in society and solve important problems."

We *trust* in people and institutions that provide stability. Providing that stability in times of rapid change requires an understanding of our stakeholders' needs, expectations, and vantage points.

PwC is one of the largest consulting firms in the world, with almost 327,000 people worldwide. The firm concentrates on creating an environment where accountability is key, fostering a spirit of trust both internally and externally. For all of our organizations, that trust takes many forms:

- trust in our commitment to deliver services on time and with the requisite quality;

- trust that we are focused on the success of our stakeholders; and

- trust to support, develop, and provide opportunities for our colleagues.

Those forms of trust are reflected in Chapter 4, where I introduced you to *The Power of Trust*. Core principles in that book's analysis include demonstrating competence, reflecting genuinely altruistic motives, and having the means to deliver on promises.[1]

Even well before March 2020, PwC, like many similar businesses, recognized the need to become more nimble in its approach to its work for its clients and its relationships with its people. In addition, it was advising clients on how to do the same. Covid just put all of those efforts into hyperdrive.

Julia Lamm is a Consulting Solutions Principal in PwC's Workforce Transformation Practice. Lamm oversees Human Capital Consulting work for PwC's financial services clients globally, which means thousands of people count on her for perspective and guidance. She spends the majority of her time helping companies around the globe manage their respective workforce. She helps them figure out how their current and future employees:

- think about work,
- act while at work,
- expect to gain from their work, and
- drive value at work.

Drawing such conclusions about current employees requires more than just your typical employee-satisfaction survey. Spotting and responding to likely trends years down the road takes lots of data, loads of experience, and a highly polished crystal ball.

Lamm leverages her background in both journalism and public relations as she investigates and analyzes the issues facing PwC's clients. She studied at University of North

Carolina – Chapel Hill, Peking University, and the Stern School of Business at New York University, honing her analytic and communication skills. Because Lamm sits on the External Advisory Board of Stern's Center for the Future of Management, she is steeped in conversations about the future of how we all work. She has probably spent more time thinking about what *your* future employment will look like than you have. Most importantly, she brings to the conversation a clear vision and an enthusiastic optimism for tackling tough issues. She isn't afraid to ask provocative questions and posit challenging options.

Lamm notes that issues that arise, even a pandemic, hit regions of the world differently. At the start of 2023, the big issue in the United States in the aftermath of Covid was inflation. For Europe, the Middle East, and Africa (EMEA), it was the energy crisis and the cost of currencies, particularly in the wake of Russia's invasion of Ukraine. In China, the top issues were restrictions to travel and exports. When it comes to issues caused by a virus, one size does not fit all. Because companies and regions experience issues differently, Lamm has learned that it's crucial to ask questions before plowing ahead based on assumptions that were true when servicing other groups. The questions we ask help us understand what people need in order to grow, how they need to grow specifically as a team, and how we can help them become more innovative.

CHALLENGING YOUR TALENT STRATEGY

Lamm has spent many years, well before Covid, focusing on how companies, including her clients and PwC, can reinvent their internal talent strategy. Her team has been analyzing how quickly companies are changing and how nimble we should be to respond to those changes.

At PwC, leaders have been asking themselves for years such fundamental questions as: "Does our talent model even make sense?" That's a radical question to be asking yourself about a business model that goes back to the dawn of capitalism itself. But they recognize we're in a world where many employees don't intend to stay at an organization long enough to become an owner of the firm.

"We've been challenging ourselves for almost a decade now," Lamm says, "about whether we should resist the changes we see in the workforce or embrace them and evolve our workforce strategies to meet the trends." PwC chose to embrace the trends. (Again, swimming upstream can wear out an organization, often for little benefit.)

Many organizations have capacity constraint issues. Companies have to look for ways to leverage the talent they already have with minimal disruption to the organization. One of Lamm's clients went through a reorganization twice in eight months. That much change created tremendous strain. The *formal* growing pains involved learning new processes. The *informal* growing pains involved learning the new team's politics and who to go to for information. Being nimble doesn't mean having to reorganize the team.

At PwC, instead of looking at wholesale reorganizations, the firm developed "My+" – its reinvented people experience strategy. Years ago, PwC recognized that the firm's people should have more autonomy over how and when they complete their work. For decades, many business consultants' weeks involved flying to a client's location on Sunday night, flying home on Thursday night, and working in their local office on Friday. Many new joiners are less attracted to that model. The firm wants its people to feel more empowered to own their careers, even if that means their entire career won't be spent at PwC. Lamm feels the program has been a big success at building trust between the firm and its people.

Moreover, those entering the workforce likely want a greater sense of mobility within the organization. In order to provide that level of flexibility and still meet clients' needs, PwC has been recruiting for skill sets rather than for particular roles. Lamm has been encouraging clients to do the same. If someone has the raw talent, you can train them on particular tasks.

One aspect of My+ has been to give people stretch roles outside of their comfort zones. The firm intentionally puts people in situations where they need to develop new skills or apply their existing skills to radically different problems. Both goals foster the kind of growth that can be critical to the individual's own success and the health of the firm. But change can have a severely negative impact on productivity.

DEVELOPING YOUR TEAM'S SKILLS AND INSTINCTS

Once you have challenged and refined your organization's structure, you need to determine how to develop the team. To do so, consider four opportunities:

1. creating clear learning paths and opportunities;
2. building efficiencies within those paths;
3. promoting collaborative behaviors; and
4. developing innovative instincts, both as individuals and as a team.

1. Creating Learning Paths and Opportunities

Lamm is in the unique position to see not just what is happening at her own firm, but how those same issues are playing out at her clients' organizations. She has seen clients help their professionals expand their skills sets using tools embedded in their software for managing human capital.

The big human resources tech providers deliver to clients software that helps track the hours worked by contract workers and professionals who bill their time to clients, such as lawyers, accountants, asset management firms, and consultants generally. Obviously, a software that tracks how much time someone bills in a given week is also tracking how much additional capacity that person may have available for other work.

It has always been the case that an individual manager who is aware that one of her team-members has low "utilization" rates could assign that person more work. That only worked, however, if the manager was tracking her team's performance closely and if that manager knows of other such work in the department that needs to be done. Working in small groups, the ability to shift work is limited.

Unlike an individual manager, however, many human capital management (HCM) tools can enable greater transparency over who is busy and who is not, and what skills people have relative to different roles. PwC has built an "Internal Talent Marketplace" that matches work that needs to be done anywhere in the firm with people with the requisite skills.

The added benefit goes beyond one of scale and impacts not only the organization's profitability, but the opportunities available to the employees. HCM software, if used correctly, can build a "skills taxonomy" for employees, showing their range of talents beyond just their job history. For instance, the software can show if someone has not just HR training, but specific experience in recruiting, learning and development, HR management, or consulting.

For some of these software tools, both the employee and manager get to assess the level of the employee's skills. When a manager is looking to meet a short-term staffing need, the HCM software can provide that manager a list of people at the company with both the available time and the requisite level of skill. Employees can enter into the database opportunities of interest to them, which increases their chance to be selected when the need arises.

The goal isn't to move people into a new permanent role. It's to give the organization a chance to use its employees' time well, and employees the chance to explore new areas of the organization without having to leave their current full-time assignment.

This could sound like a nightmare for employees who would be worried they will never have a moment's rest at work. In reality, however, it provides employees with the opportunity to expand their exposure to other areas of the company, network more broadly, and show off their skill set, all without the risk and hassle that would be involved in applying for a new full-time role. Now that's nimble.

2. Building Efficiencies within Those Paths

Life in the New Nimble, by definition, means we are faced with responding to constant shifting priorities, demands, and realities. According to Lamm, many of her clients are saying, "Enough!" They are saturated from a change perspective and have too much going on. They seek her advice on how to rethink how they are prioritizing their issues. What should they stop doing or consolidate with other initiatives? "How do we say 'no' to things?" has become a common question from her clients.

According to Lamm, a leader has to be able to say, "Enough is enough." "Saying 'no' to an idea is a powerful leadership tool," she says. Something has to come off of the plate of the employees. "You can't put more on people who are already stretched.

You can't steal capacity from people's free time. Letting people know you are focused on their workload fosters psychological safety for everyone."

Many clients are seeking a more disciplined approach to projects. They are creating the infrastructure for developing "change management" professionals. They are training more people in the organization to be change champions. How do you adapt your behaviors and your processes to demonstrate that you are open to trying new things?

Learners look for new ways to do things.

For consultants like Lamm, the "things" her clients have to accomplish are usually complex projects that need effective managers. Finding more efficient ways to manage projects helps organizations leverage talent, which, in turn, helps to decrease the volume of work on everyone's plate and reduce what senior leaders need to say "no" to.

Many of Lamm's clients are in the financial services sector. She advises their technology teams on how to develop their project management skills and instincts. The big push in project management in the last few years is converting from a classic "waterfall" approach to software development to an "Agile" approach.

The "waterfall" approach involves three steps.

1. The tech team interviews its internal clients extensively to understand the needs and objectives.

2. The team hunkers down to craft and code the perfect solution.

3. The team presents its finished product to the client and moves on to the next project.

To work efficiently, this model assumes that:

- the initial conversation was complete and that the tech team and its client understood each other fully and accurately;

- the client's needs and business would remain static between when the conversation took place and when the finished product would be delivered months later;

- the software or hardware would function as designed; and

- any unforeseen consequences of using the product won't outweigh the benefits.

Now, tech solution providers approach problems more commonly from an "Agile," iterative process. They develop solutions in stages, checking in along the way to make sure the objectives they thought were clear at the time, were, in fact, the objectives the client was trying to meet. They reassess and adapt in stages as they move forward. There are many Agile formats developed by academics and business consulting firms. Depending on whose methodology a team follows, there are 4, 6, or 10 stages in the Agile process. There are "scrum masters" who guide specific teams as project managers, and "Agile coaches," who are experienced scrum masters who can apply Agile principles across an organization.

Regardless of the titles and the jargon, the number or steps or names of the phases, Agile development means building something in an iterative process. Basically, it's the way your grandmother made soup.

Grandma asked what you wanted for dinner (sometimes). She pulled a recipe off the shelf or from memory. She added what she needed and tested it along the way. Sometimes she let you test it. Then she added more salt, more broth, more oregano, more thyme, until it worked the way it was supposed to. And grandma believed in "fast fail."[2] If something wasn't right, she'd try to salvage it, but not for too long. If she couldn't get it to work after a few tries, out it went. It wasn't going on the table if it wasn't right. Grandma didn't know it at the time, but she was an excellent scrum master.

The Agile approach, where you schedule regular check-ins with the end user, works well in the structured environment of developing incredibly precise technology solutions. Applying it to other aspects of our work world requires a bit more nuance. When we're considering hiring processes, staffing needs, and evolving client demands, we need to factor in external factors such as changing market conditions, changing economic environments, and global political developments.

Instead of running marathons, organizations are learning to be nimble by running a series of sprints. An Agile approach may take longer, but it results in a better finished product.

What it means to be Agile, or nimble, in any given situation, evolves. For those areas of business that aren't as precise as software development, the "change management" process requires more finesse. While the software developers may need training in project management skills, according to Lamm, others might need training in communication skills. Many managers may need to learn to engage employees better, which requires being more nimble in the moment. She believes that "return to the office" may be a prime example.

3. Promoting Collaborative Behaviors

Lamm had one insurance company client that had installed a technology solution but wasn't seeing the anticipated results. To make the client's team more nimble, she had to help the client's team members change their mindset about using the tool. She worked closely with the team to see how they were using the system and realized the challenges. Lamm and her team developed a course called "Leading through Change," which helped the client feel comfortable taking chances and celebrate innovative behaviors. To support that learning, they created a "community of interest" where the client's team could collaborate and share ideas about the type of work they were doing. The ability to cooperate was facilitated by the fact that they were all used to working closely together, face-to-face, in the same physical space. Those opportunities may become rarer in the New Nimble.

Working remotely is one of the chief issues that can impact creativity and innovation going forward, according to Lamm. If companies want to become or remain nimble, they likely need innovative ideas and energy.

Organic collaboration can be much harder to achieve in a virtual environment, according to Lamm. We don't "bump into people" online and say, "Do you have a few minutes? I need to bounce an idea off of you." Instead, out of respect, we know we should look at people's calendars, find a time that works for both of us, and see if they're actually still free or if their schedule shifted. Then we'll send a meeting invitation. In the meantime, we think to ourselves, "Never mind. Would have loved their input but it's taking a lot of effort to schedule time together." Or, worse yet, we have forgotten what we wanted to talk to them about anyway.

If the virtual meetings do happen, they're usually wedged in between other meetings. We've all had plenty of virtual meeting that ended with one or more participants saying, "Well, I've got to jump. I'm late for my next meeting." The unstated but necessary follow-up to that comment can be, "I won't have time to look at my notes or think about this topic when this call ends.

I may not get to that until much later in the day or week, if at all, before our next call on the topic." As a result, the creative energy that might have produced an innovative approach is lost. The extra few minutes of chit-chat at the end of an in-person meeting, when synapses are firing, and issues and ideas are just starting to gel aren't available. Efficiency or expedience trumps creativity.

By the end of the first year of Covid, organizations were already instituting "no camera Fridays" for virtual meetings, to give everyone a break from having to be camera-ready for an 8:00 a.m. meeting. Some changes are handed down as rules. Others evolve from an organization's culture. Because some form of a hybrid work environment is here to stay, we all need to find ways to promote in-person interactions or manage our remote interactions in a way that provides the mental space for creative thinking. I've included some thoughts on this later in the Takeaways section.

4. Developing Innovative Instincts Both as Individuals and as a Team

"Being nimble in the future, means creating an innovative culture now," Lamm asserts. She works on behalf of many financial services companies, including insurance companies. "Insurance as an industry is far more innovative than many might expect," she says, "but it doesn't necessarily have that reputation." As a result, it can be hard to attract the most innovative talent. In short, insurance isn't a "sexy" industry, and if you can't attract the right talent, you could have a harder time becoming more nimble.

The insurance industry has been combating this challenge on two fronts.

The well-established companies are implementing innovative ways of managing and assessing insurance claims to attract talent to the firm. For instance, they are piloting a drone program (pardon the pun). They use drones to assess property damage after a major incident. In some natural disasters, there are an enormous number of claims filed and an enormous geographic area for individual claims representatives to assess. Sending in drones to confirm the extent of damages to a broad area allows the claims representatives to draw inferences about the extent of damages and reimburse claimants more quickly.

It's newer technology and requires updated data inference tools, which can be intriguing to the kind of process and technology junkies the firm seeks to recruit. In addition, the initiative helps provide great talking points for recruiters when on college campuses for career fairs.

Newer business models are also disrupting the industry. In the last few years, more than 50 insuretech companies have launched. They combine insurance know-how with technology like artificial intelligence (AI) and data science to make it easier for consumers to apply for insurance and for the company to process claims as they are filed. The long-standing insurance brands will either innovate to address these new players in the market or will provide their own alternative services in this niche. The nascent insuretech companies will only continue to grow as new ways to apply technology to the industry are uncovered.

Being more innovative allows you to be more nimble in response to change. It also requires two philosophies to be successful.

First, your organization's compensation structure has to reward a "trial and error" approach. If your performance review process rewards "playing it safe" rather than taking even modest, calculated risks, you will never attract the kind of talent that innovates.

Second, you have to encourage fast-fail approaches, where people are encouraged to try something new, but to walk away fairly quickly if it isn't working. There is no "throwing good money after bad" in the fast-fail world.

Organizations should find ways to teach their people to have a curious mindset. Some people believe that if you change people's mindset you will change their behavior. Having coached people for almost three decades now, I know it's the opposite. If you help people to adopt different, specific behaviors, it will ultimately change their mindset. (See Chapter 4 regarding Aristotle's theory on developing moral virtue.) It's a long road to get people to "think about" being healthy and "visualize" their healthier selves. It's easier, and more productive, to get them to practice a new behavior of walking a mile every day and eating an apple instead of a bag of chips.

To help our colleagues adopt a more inquisitive mindset we should teach them to ask more questions. As they hear the responses to those questions and experience the benefit of knowing the additional information, the rewards of the behavior will prompt them to continue growing in this area.

Lamm has had the benefit of watching a wide array of companies in different industries tackle this challenge. She has seen companies take either formal or informal ways of fostering innovation. The most successful companies do both.

Formal practices to foster innovation:

Some companies have created "innovation centers," physical spaces on site at the company where people can get together and share ideas. The spaces are usually cool and funky with movable walls and places where you can showcase work that people are doing. (In Chapter 4, I shared how Matt van Geldere of Thunes hired "workplace experience managers" to help employees experience value and benefit from coming into the office.) Instead of requiring people to come to the office, entice them to the office by making it a positive, valuable experience.

One of Lamm's clients created its innovation space just outside the company's cafeteria and hosted "lunch & learn" events that brought people together. The spaces were highly visible, and the company posted the ideas creatively like at a middle-school science fair (but with better graphics). That visibility and celebration of innovation helped energize employees to be more creative.

To crowdsource ideas, PwC held a week-long event for the global team of one practice group to talk about what clients were facing and generate ideas to solve those client challenges. At the end of the week, the firm picked the leading idea and invested resources into developing it into a workable solution.

Human history has proven that we all only engage in the activities where we are rewarded. That's not selfish or Machiavellian; it's just human nature. If your organization wants to promote creativity, you'll need to assess your rewards programs to see how well it encourages innovation. If you want to go one step further, you'll actually include mention of being creative in managers' performance goals.

Informal practices that support innovation:

The informal opportunities to encourage innovation are endless and usually defy being categorized. They require an

openness to both teaching and learning that are hard to rep-
licate, but that make the real difference in an organization's
culture of learning. Grandma never sat you down to show
you when to add the oregano to the soup or how to sauté
the garlic just right. You watched, and asked, and listened,
and learned.

It's well known in corporate "learning and development" circles that 10% of learning happens in formal classes; 20% of learning happens in formal mentoring relationships. And 70% happens on the job. What does "on the job" now mean if we aren't in the same room? How do we invite people to attend meetings or observe an interaction with a client?

Overall, Lamm is an optimist about the future of work. "There is tremendous creativity and innovation right now in how we approach our work lives," she notes. "We should identify what options are right for our organization and keep an open mind as to how we execute on those options."

TAKEAWAYS

Being nimble in a fast-changing environment requires helping your team members to grow, giving them the space and the opportunity to collaborate effectively, and helping them feel comfortable to innovate with minimal personal risk.

Many organizations I have worked with have robust professional development plans for their people. And some of those firms and companies actually use those plans. Many, however, are robust on paper but rarely implemented in reality. Ultimately, we are each responsible for our own professional development. Organizations can put wonderful programs and opportunities in front of their teams, but it's up to the individual to leverage those opportunities. You don't owe it to your team members to make sure they actually invest in themselves. You do, however, owe it to your organization to make sure you are developing the most talented, nimble, effective workforce possible. Therefore, as a manager, business owner, or leader, however you define your role, part of your job is to create a culture where learning is valued, supported, accessed easily, promoted, and celebrated.

In your performance reviews with your team, how often do you ask about what professional develop opportunities your team members leveraged in the last performance cycle? What questions are on their performance review form regarding their development? Do you treat those questions as just boxes to be checked off, or do you ask the follow-up questions that show you believe the person's development matters?

"Fixed" versus "Growth" Mindset

A lot has been written about the difference between a "fixed mindset" and a "growth mindset," so I'll touch on it only briefly here.

People with a fixed mindset about a particular talent believe they have a fixed skill set in that area. They know what they are good at and enjoy the feeling of success that comes with continued success. They also are convinced they are *not* good at other things and are incapable of becoming more proficient at those skills. They don't try to expand their skills because doing so will require too much work and will likely be futile.

People with a growth mindset believe they are capable of learning new skills sets and are eager to tackle new opportunities.

A single individual may have a growth mindset in one area of their life and a fixed mindset around another area. I practiced law for almost a decade before becoming a communications consultant. Many of my coaching clients are lawyers, mostly at large, global law firms. By and large, they have a growth mindset about their legal skills. They are eager to take on the next big merger or defend their client in increasingly complex litigation matters. Those same attorneys, however, may have a fixed mindset when it comes to building their book of business. Many have limited experience bringing in new clients. They look at their firm's rainmakers with both awe and bewilderment. They view the ability to "sell" as something foreign. They think it's not just outside their comfort zone, it's outside the realm of possible skills for them to learn.

Having a fixed mindset gets in the way of being nimble. In *Selling Your Expertise: The Mindset, Strategies, and Tactics of Successful Rainmakers*,[3] Robert Chen writes "A practical way to begin developing a growth mindset is to see yourself as a learner rather than a performer. Performers look to get things right. Learners focus on improving their abilities."[4]

Managing the Workday

If you're like many people with workdays that are too tightly packed with meetings, here are two approaches you can try to become more efficient and effective.

The first approach is a classic time-management technique. If possible, block 15 minutes on your calendar after each meeting. It creates mental space and some emotional relief when you aren't feeling so rushed.

The second approach is a communication skills technique. If you only have a few minutes at the end of a meeting, take a quick look at your notes from the meeting. Chances are you wrote down a lot of nouns; we tend to write down the concrete, tangible words when taking notes. Add a verb in with the nouns. If you have a verb and a noun together, you have a full sentence, and the concept will mean more to you when you look at it in a few days.

Conclusion

We set the tone as leaders about how we value personal growth. What growth opportunities have your team members seen you participate in that set the expectations for them?

Being nimble isn't intuitive for most people. It's a learned behavior. In the next chapter, we'll talk about how you can continue to ask the right questions of your team members to make sure they hone those skills for themselves.

Questions for you and your team to consider:

1. How do we qualify and quantify the talents and skills of our team members? How do we find opportunities to leverage those talents and skills?

2. How does the size and nature of our organization allow us to shift resources as needed?

3. To what extent is our organization already Agile in terms of how we approach projects?

4. What parameters can we put in place around scheduled virtual meetings that create the casual, unstructured time that the human brain needs for creativity to flourish?

5. How can we develop awareness among our team members regarding the need for collaborative time and space? For those team members who are always remote, how do we bring them into the conversation more organically?

6. Do we feel rewarded for promoting innovation? What kind of reward would we need to prompt us to move being innovative higher on our agenda? How could we approach our organization about putting such rewards in place?

CHAPTER 6

Seek "Meaningful Knowledge"

Institutions of higher education are facing challenges on many fronts today, including:

- declining enrollment,

- increasing costs,

- clashes regarding what content is appropriate to discuss on a campus, and

- attacks on the very value of a college degree.

These and many other issues make managing a university a daily exercise in evaluating complex information, balancing competing interests, and making quick decisions. And universities operate in a more public forum than most companies. When students, faculty, staff, and alumni choose to air their positions and their occasional grievances on social media, they only heighten the challenge.

A liberal arts education has historically involved learning to ask better questions, thinking critically about the information gleaned, and responding thoughtfully. A public company might focus on meeting quarterly projections. By contract, an academic institution, especially a liberal arts university, is supposed to keep its eye on the big picture, seek eternal truths, and take a holistic approach to analyzing and understanding the human experience. Thoughtful, discerned responses take time and deliberation, neither of which is valued on the nightly news' "viewers' polls" or in twitchy-fingered Twitter responses. And, yet, colleges and universities, too, must learn to be nimble in their responses to events of the moment. How do you play the long game while responding to daily disruptions? How do you keep playing chess when the rest of the world has opted for Whack-A-Mole?

Real change in education happens slowly, over generations rather than years. When we look back on the pandemic, we will see the most radical shift in education since the advent of the computer. Overnight – specifically over the night of March 13, 2020 – teachers everywhere from Fordham Law School in New York to Kuhio Elementary School in Honolulu were told to transition to virtual learning or pack it in. Covid was the meteor that impacted the education landscape in an instant and forever. The dinosaurs are gone, and the new, nimble world is here to be dealt with.

While many organizations feel like they are finally coming out of the pandemic, institutions of higher education are realizing they are only beginning to feel the effects. The disruption caused by the pandemic involved not just having to convert classes to online learning, and "de-densify" dorms and classrooms. Those challenges will turn out to have been the easy part. Universities will need to remain nimble in the coming years as they respond to a changing demographics and the evolving demands of those seeking a higher education. It's worth looking at how one university managed through the pandemic, and how it is rethinking itself and the needed changes in higher education in the coming years.

Profile: Salve Regina University (Higher Ed) – "We Got This"

High on the bluffs overlooking the Atlantic Ocean in Newport, Rhode Island sits the 80-acre campus of Salve Regina University. For 75 years, the Sisters of Mercy, an order of Roman Catholic nuns, has operated the small, liberal arts school that includes undergraduate and Master's degree programs in dozens of fields of study.

Throughout its history, Salve's core mission has been more informed by the charism of the Sisters of Mercy than by the privilege of its neighborhood. It has attracted and served students of all faiths and backgrounds. Salve's Mission Statement ends with, "The University encourages students to work for a world that is harmonious, just, and merciful." The faculty and staff at Salve dedicate themselves to helping students prepare to work toward achieving that world. It requires cultivating students' self-awareness and perspective on their role in society.

Dr. Kelli Armstrong, the eighth president of the university, and its first lay leader, began her tenure in mid-2019. She brought to Salve 15 years of experience in various senior leadership roles at Boston College, another Catholic university based in the Northeast. That experience helped her hone her decisiveness as a leader and the instincts to build the kind of collaborative community necessary in an academic environment. Her grounding in leadership, and the culture established by the Sisters of Mercy, have allowed Armstrong to guide Salve through the pandemic and through other less dramatic but also important challenges in her four years at the helm.

I joined the Board of Trustees of Salve in the fall of 2019 and participated in only one board meeting in person before we shifted to virtual meetings like everyone else in the world. Although I had been a high school English teacher for a few years between college and law school, I had never been part of a leadership team of a school before. I hadn't appreciated the constant innovation needed in an academic institution.

DURING THE PANDEMIC

Early in her tenure as president of the university, Dr. Armstrong began meeting with faculty and staff to understand their roles, their goals, their strengths, and their motivations. One early meeting was with Jim Ludes, the director of the Pell Center for International Relations and Public Policy, based at Salve. The center, named after Claibourne Pell, the long-serving U.S. Senator from Rhode Island, runs programming on a wide array of public policy topics. One signature project of the center is *Story in the Public Square*, the weekly PBS show that brings audiences "to the intersection of storytelling and public policy." The show has won six Telly Awards for its interviews, and is hosted by Ludes and veteran journalist G. Wayne Miller.

Prior to his 11 years at Salve, Ludes had been the Executive Director of the American Security Project and had worked for Senator John Kerry.

As reports of a novel respiratory virus in China began to circulate, Ludes asked Armstrong if the university's business continuity plan was ready for a pandemic. The then Dean of Students, Malcolm Smith, had an Emergency Management Team (EMAT), which included members of the university's Health & Safety, Food Service, Facilities, Academic Affairs, and Security offices. The group had plans for major storms and power outages, and even for public health emergencies. The group had identified the university's "essential employees" long before that term became part of the common vernacular.

Ludes joined Smith's team in early 2020. Two months later, on Friday, March 13, 2020, the Rhode Island Department of Health (RIDOH) ordered Salve and all universities to cease conducting in-person classes and to send all students home. Salve needed leaders to manage the response to an event far bigger than anyone had anticipated.

Like all universities, Salve was uncertain how long the shutdown would remain in effect. At first, Salve's leaders thought the school would be operating remotely for two weeks, then, for the rest of the semester. As it became apparent they would need to operate differently in the fall, Armstrong tapped Ludes to develop a plan.

Others at the university created a "Salve's Got This" campaign. As noted earlier, acting with mercy is at the core of Salve's mission. The faculty and administrators in Academic Affairs figured out the details of getting classes up and running virtually. In the meantime, volunteers from across the campus community called every single Salve student at home to see how they and their families were faring. They asked what the students needed in order to participate in classes remotely, and just to check in on their mental well-being.

Salve had to figure out how to remain "open," including defining what *open* might mean. The guidance from the state wasn't particularly helpful. The RIDOH was appropriately focused on "maintaining health." Most organizations, Salve included, were focused on "maintaining health while still functioning."

EMAT created a tiered triage grid to allow them to make decisions quickly as the situation warranted. The grid incorporated responses based on two major factors: the level of social distancing required by the state, and revenue coming in from tuition. Although the majority of Salve students are on financial aid, Salve, like most private universities, depends on tuition revenue to manage operations. Only the largest and oldest universities have the kind of endowment that allows them to operate without keeping a constant eye on revenue.

The triage grid looked at more than 30 aspects of running the university including core elements like classes and housing, and key events like move-in dates and sporting events.

EMAT evaluated the impact on each event or element based on state requirements regarding social distancing. It then color-coded how the university would respond to each situation based on whether revenues would be as budgeted (green), down by 20% (yellow), or down by 50% (red). The grid included a plan of action for a particular event or university function as the situation warranted. The leadership team was able to use the grid to make decisions quickly in a fluid environment. The team had to assess how moving an event into the RED mode would cascade through other elements of the university.

Assessing all of these elements created what Ludes refers to as "a strong desire for meaningful knowledge," an apt goal in an academic institution. "As we were putting our plans in place, we started to refer to 'preliminary' decisions, until we realized all of our decisions were preliminary because they kept changing as the quality of information improved."

Although they were able to implement a plan, Ludes notes that didn't guarantee everything would go smoothly. "There was no conflict at the meetings," he notes, "but there was lots of 'shock and awe' as we discussed worst-case scenarios. We were definitely naïve about the situation." The unprecedented level of uncertainty created a reluctance to act, which is certainly true for organizations profiled in other chapters in this book.

In Chapter 3, regarding Memorial Health, we saw how a "command and control" structure worked for some organizations. In my limited exposure to the inner workings of a university, I have been surprised at how few people seem used to taking orders. Most decisions seem driven by consensus. Armstrong joined the meetings as necessary when a group needed someone to make the final decisions, but EMAT did all the heavy lifting on the analysis and planning.

In fact, at one point, Ludes and Smith told their new president that it would be best if she didn't come to the meetings. They felt that her presence was stifling the conversation as everyone would wait to see what she thought. They wouldn't want to contribute ideas in case she was firm about going in one direction and they had already voiced a contrary position. As a result, the group wasn't getting the creativity, candor, and disagreement it needed to produce the best solutions. Armstrong readily agreed and got out of the way. She indicated she always felt welcome to attend when she wanted to. However, she knew her absence from the meetings freed the group to make many of the basic decisions and freed her to concentrate elsewhere. Nevertheless, when it was time to make the really tough calls, the decision landed with her.

At one point, the baseball team was ready to go to a tournament in Florida. Team members were leaving that afternoon, and the athletic director wanted to approve them to go. The group debated it at a meeting that Armstrong attended. A few hours after the meeting, Armstrong made the call to not allow the team to go because of the risk to the athletes' health. If they got stuck in Florida, it would create major complications for everyone. Shortly thereafter, all of the other schools that had planned to attend made the same call. If the Salve Seahawks had gone, they would have had no one to compete against.

Ultimately, Salve managed through the pandemic with alacrity. The school was fully open and operational for the 2020 fall semester with all classes taught in a hybrid format. The infection and transmission rates were exceptionally low. Tuition revenue declined, but not dramatically.

Ludes credits the school's success at managing through the pandemic to people's trust in each other and in their ability to think through the issues clearly and prioritize effectively.

He notes, "You have to have confidence that you are making the best decisions with all of the info you have on hand." His three suggestions for success apply equally well to the other challenges the university is now facing.

1. Don't get paralyzed by the enormity of the situation.

2. Keep your head on a swivel so that you can change course if you get more info.

3. Debrief to assess whether your decisions were the best in the moment and how they could have been improved.

While EMAT handled the pandemic, President Armstrong was able to focus on Salve's strategic initiatives. The school had committed to developing its new "Salve Compass" program to reorient the school's curriculum, described later in this chapter. "We had committed to a certain growth and evolution as an institution," Nancy Schreiber, Salve's Provost commented. "If Kelli had gotten wrapped up in the details of the Covid response, she couldn't have kept that momentum going. Sure, the pandemic slowed us down a bit. But we kept moving. Now, as we come out of the pandemic, we'll be able to launch new initiatives, a bit delayed, but still moving forward."

BEYOND THE PANDEMIC

The 2020s will prove to be a pivotal decade for higher education in the United States. For academia, Covid played the role of only an intro-level course on change management. The advanced courses will require greater concentration, better information, and increased nimbleness. Though Covid was bad, demographic and societal changes will have more significant impacts on how our colleges and universities will function and train the minds of the future. Our schools will need to learn to seek meaningful knowledge on many fronts.

Demographics

Starting in 2025, there will be a precipitous drop in the number students graduating from high school in the United States. Some estimates suggest the college-going population will drop by as much as 15% between 2025 and 2029.[1] The decline is due primarily to the significant and sustained drop in birthrates starting in 2008 when the financial crisis hit. The numbers will have an enormous impact on college admissions. In addition, the pandemic caused many students to delay going to college for a year or two. Many education experts believe that phenomenon may continue even now that the pandemic is over. The combination of these two factors has caused many small liberal arts schools like Salve to rethink how they recruit students. They will have to learn to accommodate and create programs attractive to first-year college students who are 21 or 22 instead of the traditional 18-year-olds.

College recruiting programs have never run on autopilot. They are highly data-driven and analytical in their approach to attracting students. The college recruiting industry is sophisticated and has put in place elements that have allowed them to succeed. College fairs, recruiting schedules, feeder high schools, standardized testing schedules, and *U.S. News* rankings have all played a consistent role in college admissions for decades. Transitions from paper applications to online platforms like Naviance and innovations like the "common app" were surface, not substantive, changes to how colleges recruited and evaluated students.

Colleges have had to respond to economic downturns before, and their campuses have often led the way on reacting to social justice issues. Neither of those factors has created the kind of threat posed by such a huge shift in the core demographics that will take place in the coming years. In the early 2020s, colleges had already started to reach out to high school first-year students and sophomores rather than targeting juniors. As a result, the decreased size of their target audience is already impacting colleges and universities.

This isn't the first time that a demographic shift has impacted higher education. In the 1970s, a decrease in the high-school graduation numbers caused a shift in college recruiting practices. This time, however, will be different and create a more existential crisis for many institutions.

In the 1970s, well below a third of high school graduates continued their formal education. There was a huge untapped market of students who hadn't previously considered or hadn't been able to go to college. Around the same time, gaining a college degree became viewed as the best avenue to better jobs and improved financial security.

According to Jim Fowler, Salve's Vice President of Enrollment Management, "In the 1970s families started to realize that getting an advanced degree was the road into the middle class and beyond." Therefore, when the overall number of high school graduates started to decline, colleges and universities started to appeal to the vast population of high school graduates who previously wouldn't have applied to college at all.

Now, however, more than 65% of high school graduates participate in some form of post-secondary education. It's unlikely that percentage will grow substantially. "The market is saturated at this point," notes Fowler.

According to Fowler, who has more than 30 years in college admissions, "The way you remain nimble in this situation is first to accept that you must change. You can't just sit back and say, 'We believe in the value of higher education,' and everything will be OK. Your complacency will be your downfall. You can't just ride out the storm."

While elite schools will continue to have their pick of top students, smaller, less well known schools will suffer as their traditional pool of candidates shrinks, and many local colleges will either close or radically reinvent themselves and redefine their mission.

Societal Changes

In addition to the demographic cliff facing colleges and universities, two societal changes are impacting how universities function. First, there are challenges to the very purpose of higher education. Second, students are entering university with increased levels of mental health challenges and decreased coping skills. They are struggling to solve their own problems.

Society, or at least the college-bound part of society, has been rethinking the purpose and value of higher education overall because of its cost, the access to learning outside of institutional settings, and, some would argue, a general impatience with the learning process.

Fowler notes, "Until the last decade, the intentionality around going to college had to do with intellectual enrichment and the general sense that if I got a better education it would lead to a better career and economic prospects broadly. Now, incoming students – and their parents – are demanding to see a direct link between the course of study and the ability to get that first job." In a way, they are evaluating the college experience from a more tactical rather than strategic approach. According to Fowler, "They are looking to college as a job-training program. They want to see if college can teach them how to write a professional email and how to interact with people in a professional setting. If they can't see that direct link, they're reluctant to make the investment."

This need to articulate their value in such concrete, mercenary terms is a radical change and challenge for schools that have long identified their purpose as standing for intangibles. Consider some typical school mottos:

- "God & Truth" (Colgate University),

- "Arts, Knowledge, & Truth" (University of Michigan),

- "Knowledge & Wisdom" (University of Mississippi – Ole Miss), and

- "The Wind of Freedom Blows" (Stanford University).[2]

Salve's goal of helping students create a world that is "harmonious, just, and merciful" doesn't exactly link directly to any job title I can think of. Translating that branding into something that resonates with students with more pragmatic sensibilities will require some adept adjustments, a willingness to try new things, and an openness to knowing you will fail at some of those efforts.

As previously noted, Salve is responding by introducing the "Salve Compass" initiative, which aligns the school's undergraduate curriculum with professional competencies. The goal isn't to abandon the liberal arts and veer toward becoming a vocational school. Rather, the Compass will challenge professors in all disciplines to help students see more directly the link between the knowledge and skills they are gaining and how those skills come into play in the real world. For Salve, the added focus will be on clarifying what it means to get a "Mercy" education.

In Loco Parentis *Has a Whole New Meaning*

Another societal change universities are dealing with is a student body that is having an increasingly difficult time speaking for itself. Students were reporting higher levels of mental health needs even before Covid gave all of us the occasional panic attack. Many schools are dealing with parents who intervene for their kids on matters that, in the past, students would have handled themselves.

Most students continue to make it through their entire undergraduate academic without one of their parents calling the school to complain about the level of coursework or the food in the cafeteria. But when parents do contact the school on a relatively minor issue, they call the president's office directly. Apparently, if a parent is taking the time to call, the parent doesn't think the issue is minor. Those calls cause tremendous inefficiencies, particularly at small colleges. The president's office must quickly direct the issue to the relevant dean, and the dean has to investigate the issue and repair the problem.

More importantly, a call from a parent to a university on behalf of their adult child is a troubling sign of how prepared the student is for adult life. From a legal perspective, for much of the twentieth century, universities were thought to function *in loco parentis*, meaning standing in the role of the parent. This concept wasn't just about housing young adults. *In loco parentis* required that schools not only educated students, but were responsible for their moral development. That legal doctrine allowed schools to enforce a wide array of codes of conduct that today seem antiquated. The doctrine fell away in the later part of the last century. Now, for some students, the university doesn't need to step into that role because the parents never quite leave the child's side.

Because of the delayed social skills among so many students, universities have become more nimble in the way they help students through the undergraduate experience.

Salve is responding to this growing societal issue by moving to a professional first-year advisor model. Almost all colleges have some form of advisor program for first-year students. The advisor is usually a faculty member who is supposed to meet with the student a few times each year to see how the student is progressing and if there are any problems. For decades, that role was known as an "Academic Advisor." As that advising has, of necessity, started to include elements of counseling, professionals with specific training beyond providing academic direction are needed.

As the incidences of mental health issues have increased across the country, and have spiked since Covid, schools have realized that many faculty members either aren't equipped to be an advisor or no longer want to handle the added responsibility. As a result, some schools have hired professional advisors trained to help the students speak for themselves and learn to solve their own problems. The goal is to help the students themselves become more nimble.

It's Not about Perfection; It's about Progress

Finally, creating a more nimble workforce in a university requires acknowledging the two major players involved in academic settings – faculty and staff. According to Provost Schreiber, "Each has its own rights, privileges, and obligations."

Anyone who was either in school at the time of the pandemic or had children in school was hyperaware of how hard it was for students to adjust to remote learning. Anyone on the inside of an academic institution was also aware of how hard the adjustment was for the faculty and staff.

Although for-profit corporations are responsive to many stakeholders, their primary responsibility is to generate profits for their shareholders. Their employees are motivated by many elements, but often define their status in the organization by rank and by compensation. The staff at non-profits have other motivations, and often work side-by-side with volunteers, who sometimes do similar work for no compensation whatsoever. Universities are a unique subset within the world of non-profits.

According to Schreiber, "faculty and staff at universities each operate with their own set of motivators. The staff needs to be responsive in the moment to a situation and are held accountable through a typical hierarchical management structure. The faculty, on the other hand, act more as independent agents, responsible to their own intellectual integrity." Except for the occasional student recording a professor's comments on their phone and posting it on social media, most of the time the university has little insight into what's actually going on in a particular class.

Creating Nimble Faculty

Most non-profits are focused on solving a social problem – feeding the hungry, sheltering the homeless, caring for the unwanted. The world of higher education focuses on the growth and self-actualization of the individual. We go to school to learn to grow into our bigger, better, more complete selves. Although education is the single biggest factor in lifting an individual and a group out of poverty, that's just a huge added benefit of the immediate goal, which is the uniquely personal growth for each individual.

The focus on "learning for the sake of learning" imbues everything on an academic campus. While faculty strives for tenure, and then often seeks the accolades and notoriety that come with publishing, "getting ahead" isn't often the goal the way it is in the corporate world. As Schreiber notes, "academics only get promoted, at the most, twice in their career. The first time is when they are tenured and promoted to associate professor. The second time is if they chose to apply to become full professor."

In fact, universities sometimes struggle to get their faculty to take on roles like "department chair" or to lead a new initiative. Often the additional compensation that goes with the role doesn't begin to cover the added time commitment or the hassle of having to "manage" a group of colleagues. Time spent working on such initiatives is time taken away from that faculty member's ability to continue working on that next article or book, or work on that project in the lab.

University faculty often function more as independent contributors all aiming toward a collective goal, rather than in a traditional team model. The dozen or so professors in a university's English department, for instance, operate fairly independently from each other. They follow the same administrative protocols, but their success in their roles is largely not dependent on their colleagues' success in theirs. They might function as sounding boards for each other, but they don't "need" each other the way members of teams do.

We all knew the college or graduate school professor who was clearly delivering their lecture from the same set of notes they had used decades previously. For some instructors that was OK. Has there been that much new scholarship on Kant or James Joyce in the last few years that would lead a professor to update their analysis? Others are very innovative, looking to bring ancient texts to life by relating them to current events, but the motivation to do so is internal. There is no "hue and cry" to update syllabi about Proust or molecular biology. What a shock to the system, then, when things changed overnight.

Academia, particularly in a liberal arts setting, is known for teaching critical thinking skills, how to think through complex problems. "But when it comes to being nimble, to being innovative," Schreiber notes, "critical thinking is only half of the equation. The other half is the psychology of risk-taking." She notes that universities have to create a psychologically safe space for people to try something new and to allow room for failure. Failure doesn't have to be rewarded, but it has to be expected and tolerated in order for people to innovate. "By definition, to act nimbly means to do something you've really never done before, and to be prepared to deal with the consequences of your actions when you're not sure what they might be. That means you have to have a heightened tolerance for risk."

"The fear of failure," she notes, "isn't just about failure at a particular initiative. It's the fear that one failure will define you as a person." In other words, in an unhealthy environment, "failure" isn't just about what happens when something doesn't work; it's a label, a brand, that sticks with a person. Your project wasn't a failure; you were. "And that 'failure' label isn't just individual," Schreiber notes. "It can be institutional."

According to Schreiber, who joined the university five years ago, Salve has the pros and cons of its two defining DNA strands – an academic setting of higher ed and the Roman Catholic Church, two entities or environments with great intrinsic qualities, but not known for pivoting quickly.

That said, Schreiber notes, "Our faculty was amazing when the pandemic struck. They switched to virtual teaching as readily as everyone else in the country did." But she notes, "Like everyone else, they had no choice. If you didn't figure it out, you were out of a job." Apparently, survival instincts kick in pretty quickly during a crisis, regardless of your discipline. The true test of the university's ability to create a dynamic, innovative, and nimble teaching environment will play out over the next few years as demographic shifts upend the world of higher education.

Creating Nimble Staff

"The main issue in a crisis," Schreiber notes, "is that you have to keep moving forward. If you stop, if you freeze, you're done."

To be innovative, to be able to shift appropriately, you need to be comfortable assessing your success. "Whether an initiative worked or didn't work, you need to institutionalize a debrief process that lets you learn from both the successes and the failures. You need to go beyond both that self-congratulatory pat-on-the-back or the 'mea culpas' and opt for a 'continuous improvement process.'"

"It's not enough," Schreiber believes, "to just say 'it worked' or 'it didn't work.' You need to garner two action items out of every debrief. That's what informs your path forward as a decision-maker." She notes, "It's about asking, 'What worked? What didn't work? What would have worked better?' And, 'Why' as to each." Her goal is to help the faculty and staff feel empowered to try new ideas, to pilot new modes of teaching, and to do so with a sense that occasional failures will at the very least generate learning.

Fowler takes the same approach with regard to initiatives around enrollment. "If you believe in the value of your curriculum, you just need the right way of getting the word out about your program, or so it would seem," he says. This is where the notion of taking risks and being willing to "fast fail" discussed in other chapters comes into play in the world of academia.

Salve offers dozens of graduate level degrees and certificates. If someone is considering applying for a Master's degree program, they are clearly thinking strategically about their career and their educational and professional goals. While some high school students apply to college because it's what's expected or because it's what everyone else is doing, few people apply to a graduate program without a lot of reflection.

Salve assumed the target audience for its graduate programs would, by definition, be more intellectually motivated and more discerning about selecting the program that meets their goals. As a pilot, Fowler's team recorded a series of short, 20-minute "roundtable discussions" with professors and practitioners in some of the fields in which they offered programs.

Fowler noted, "I felt the conversations were so deep and intimate and really got to the root of how the programs work, what's offered, and the benefits. If you watched the videos, you really gained some of the intangibles you couldn't get from reading content online. We thought these would be a big hit. It turns out people would watch them for 2–3 minutes and then drop off.

We learned that even at the graduate level, people's willingness to do the research necessary to choose a program is limited."

"We had planned to create a video for each advanced degree program," Fowler said. "We gave the first few videos one recruiting cycle. The reactions were so consistent and lackluster, we abandoned the project. We assessed whether the issue was likely the format, the quality of the discussion or recording, or the concept. Ultimately, we decided it wouldn't be worthwhile to continue with the project.[3] You need to try new things, assess them, and know when to pivot."

Schreiber likes to say, "It's not about perfection. It's about progress. You don't have to score a touchdown every time you move the ball, but you have to move the ball." Schreiber believes a leader has to have the trust of the people behind her to create the sense of urgency that communicates that staying still is worse than moving. "You have to be able to explain in a compelling and emotional and logical way that staying still will lead to your demise."

TAKEAWAYS

The speed of life at the moment requires us to focus on quick solutions for the problems immediately in front of us. The focus of this book is about making quick decisions in an ever-changing environment. And, yet, this chapter, in particular, is about figuring out how to incorporate into our thinking and our evaluative process the greater truths, the more thoughtful and discerned analyses that will help us make better decisions that have a more long-lasting impact.

I referenced both Immanuel Kant and James Joyce earlier in this chapter for a reason. Their philosophies underpin the takeaways from this chapter.

Kant once said, "All our knowledge begins with the senses, proceeds then to the understanding, and ends with reason. There is nothing higher than reason." The progression is important to note.

We learn through our senses by feeling the softness of the pillow, smelling the aroma of a loaf of bread baking, or seeing a sentence like this one and taking in knowledge. We then move on to understanding, know we are about to settle in for a comfortable night, enjoy a delicious meal, or learn a new concept about being nimble.

We then end with reason, knowing that sleep helps us rejuvenate, mere sustenance can be pleasurable, and learning can help us grow.

"Reason" is the end goal of all institutions of higher learning, as is evident from the university mottos shared earlier in this chapter. Reason should also be guiding all of our decisions, whether they are the result of careful deliberation or nimble responsiveness.

Like universities, all organizations have roles with different perspectives and objectives. Our responsiveness depends on our ability to draw analogies. What roles are "staff" and what roles are "faculty" in your organization? Who are the "students" whose legitimate needs and frequent whims you try to accommodate? Who are the "parents" who aren't on your list of immediate "stakeholders" but are ever-present voices that need to be addressed? How do your "independent contributors" differ from your "team players" in terms of how you need to respond to their needs?

If you manage a sales team, your salespeople might help each other with best practices, but the performance of the person handling the "West/Central" region doesn't impact the success of their colleague overseeing the "South/Florida" region. They're like collegial members of the English Department – glad to help each other with nifty ideas, but ultimately not impacting each other's effectiveness.

If you're part of the marketing team, however, you're stepping in for each other as needed. When one person is on vacation or out sick, you're all responsible for the results of the unit. You're akin to the "staff" at the university.

Your organization has to be structured to support both types of contributions, allowing creativity and experimentation to happen in each role.

Where Kant provides guidance regarding reason, James Joyce tackles the idea of staying positive and moving forward. *Ulysses*, Joyce's most important and revered work in literary and educational settings,[4] traces one man, Leopold Bloom, as he wanders around Dublin on June 16, 1904. Joyce presents Bloom's journey on the same epic scale as Homer tracing Ulysses through the Greek isles after the Trojan Wars. On his trek, Bloom experiences the morbid and mundane, the sad and the sardonic of life in the mostly rougher parts of his city before returning home to his wife, Molly. In spite of spending most of the book sharing the grim and grimy of Leopold's life, Joyce closes *Ulysses* with the famous last line of Molly Bloom exclaiming in ecstasy, "YES! I Said YES! I Will YES!"

It's that affirmation of the triumph of the human spirit and the possibility of tomorrow that makes being nimble so important. As so many have shared in this chapter and this book so far, it's all about finding a way forward. The troubles of today or of this week or year or decade will be overcome not by complacency, not by patience, not by adherence to the status quo. We will meet the challenges of today and tomorrow by acting, by putting one foot in front of the other, and braving to take the next step. In the next chapters you will hear how others made those bold moves.

Questions for you and your team to consider:

1. Where can we seek meaningful knowledge about our industry?

2. In our industry, what change that occurred during Covid was just the precursor for a related but deeper change?

3. When we consider the way our industry approaches serving its audience, what paradigm shifts are headed our way? Where can you find that data, the meaningful knowledge, that will help us prepare for that change?

4. When we examine how we managed through either the pandemic or any other large-scale challenge:

   (a) What worked?

   (b) What didn't work?

   (c) What could have worked better?

   Can we articulate, "Why" as to each?

5. When we think about how we and our team approach a problem, how does Kant's framework apply? How did we take in information through the senses, process that information to create true understanding, and then apply reason to achieve our decision? Are we merely justifying your behaviors or are our answers legitimate?

PART III

BE BOLD

Ultimately, being nimble means taking action. We're not being nimble when we shift uncomfortably in our seats, waiting awkwardly for the situation to change. That's not leading. That's squirming.

Leading is about taking bold, decisive action, even when we know that some of our smaller steps along the way will fail. Being nimble means moving even when our movement may cause us to bump up against other forces – uncertainty in the market, challenges from those who disagree with us, the other player on the court. That's OK. We're defined by our actions more than we are by our hopes, dreams, fears, and aspirations. We're not defined by our good intentions. We're defined by what steps we take because of those intentions.

In this final part, we'll look at the actions of both teams and individuals in moments of tremendous stress. The supply chain that brings all of us the products we use every day showed both its elasticity and its ingenuity. The actions of some of our elected leaders helped hold the nation together after the January 6 insurrection. The willingness of competitors to join voices drew greater attention to a blight on our society. The actions of all of these individuals and groups required strong relationships, reliable data from the right sources, and more than a little chutzpah.

CHAPTER 7

Keep It Moving

Good things may come to those who wait, but only the things left by those who hustle.

—Abraham Lincoln

If you're not five minutes early, you're late.

—Robert Tracy – Co-Founder of Dot Foods, Inc.

Patience is a virtue. Patience helps us remain calm and reflects an inner peace and humility with our circumstances. It serves us well when things are not within our control. As discussed in Chapter 3, as leaders, we need to distinguish between those things we can control and those we cannot. While we can remain patient about those we cannot control, we need to be ready to take decisive action around those elements where we can have impact. We need to move quickly and take advantage of them efficiently. Being able to pivot when needed requires having the right relationships in place, confidence in the information coming in, and the bravery to be decisive.

PROFILE: DOT FOODS, INC. (SUPPLY CHAIN) – DELIVERING IN A CRISIS

As you're reading this, you're conscious of absorbing the content, but you're not thinking about flexing your eye muscles to move across the line or contracting your pupils to focus. You feel your chest expand as you breath in, but you can't feel the air move through the walls of your lungs to oxygenate your blood. You're conscious of your mind processing ideas, but you can't feel the synapses in your brain firing. If we were processing all of those activities, every blink, breath, and brainwave would distract and overwhelm us. We take all of those activities for granted in order to get through not just the day, but through every moment.

The same is true for the supply chains around us that get our gas to the station, our clothes on the store racks, and our food on the shelves of our local grocery store. The body of our universe has to function on an unconscious basis for us. We don't think about how we access the tools and products we need every day – until they aren't there. We don't think about the supply chain until the chain breaks.

Over the last 50 years, supply chains have become increasingly more efficient. The Great Depression was caused, in part, by companies holding too much inventory, and manufacturers creating products without an understanding of the short and long-term demand. Now, supply chains have become so efficient that product is produced on demand and arrives in days. If you ordered this book on Amazon, chances are it was printed the next day and mailed to you immediately. It didn't *exist* until after you clicked "Yes" on the button that read, "Confirm purchase." You *initiated* the supply chain for this book.

During Covid, a switch flipped, and we all became immediately and painfully aware of the supply chains that support our lives. Some rushed out to hoard toilet paper, while others stockpiled home hair dye kits. We assessed our own buying patterns and asked ourselves, "What do I use frequently and how much of it will I need for the next few weeks? Months?!" That way of thinking was new to most of us. It wasn't new, however, to the 6,000 employees of Dot Foods, Inc., the largest food redistributor in North America. What Dot experienced holds lessons for all of us in managing through a crisis.

In Chapter 2, you read about Bowery Farming, a vertical farming company producing fresh produce close to the cities where it is consumed. Bowery's aim is to shrink the supply chain, minimizing the distance to market. Dot works in a different channel of the food industry as a "re-distributor." Here's a grossly over-simplified description of how food distribution works, and Dot's role in it. Food manufacturers like Kraft or Del Monte create vast quantities of the processed foods we all consume. They want to move their product out as efficiently as possible, ideally by selling truckloads of each product. The food distribution company that delivers to your local restaurants and schools has to carry thousands of products to meet its customer needs, but doesn't want to have to tie up capital and pay for warehouse space to buy a truckload of each product. That's where Dot comes in.

Dot buys truckloads of over 125,000 products from food manufacturers. Every day, hundreds of trucks arrive at Dot's 14 distribution centers from Calgary, Alberta, to Vidalia, Georgia. Dot then delivers to local food distributors exactly what that distributor needs for the week. Hundreds of trucks arrive at Dot every day carrying a single product; hundreds of trucks go out, each with possibly thousands of products going to a customer. The loading dock at Dot's headquarters in Mt. Sterling, Illinois, is an amazing ballet of forklifts scurrying down aisles, shrink-wrap machines whirling around stacks of pallets, and loaders gingerly packing boxes into the 100-plus open truck bay doors. It's a well-choreographed dance that worked smoothly for 60 years, until March 13, 2020.

On Thursday, March 12, George Eversman, Dot's then executive Vice President for Business Development and Retail and now its president, was driving to the Lambert St. Louis airport for a flight to San Diego. He was supposed to help host more than 500 employees and their spouses at the company's Winner Circle incentive trip, set to begin the next day. When Eversman arrived at the airport, he learned via email that the Dot trip was cancelled because of concerns about the new virus everyone was talking about. The week before, Expo West, the largest exposition of natural and organic foods, had been cancelled out of concern about Covid transmission. Eversman has been in the food industry for three decades. This was the first time he recalled any large events being cancelled. When Eversman spoke that weekend with Cullen Andrews, the company's Vice President of Sales and Marketing, they discussed the rumors that state and local governments were considering closing all restaurants the following week. It seemed highly improbable. They couldn't imagine now how the entire restaurant industry could be shuttered overnight.

On Monday, both men were back at the company's corporate headquarters in Mt. Sterling, Illinois, when they received confirmation of the shutdown. Immediately, the company's senior leadership team triaged the issues and developed a plan. The first order of business was to address the crisis that was about to unfold at all of Dot's distribution centers.

As Dot's drivers arrived at customers' loading docks that day to drop off product, some customers were refusing to accept the product. That meant hundreds of trucks that had been loaded with inventory a few hours earlier would be returning to Dot's warehouses full instead of empty. At the same time, customers were calling to cancel orders for the coming weeks, uncertain of their own need for product as their clients – restaurants and event-venues – were being told they had to close. That meant those trucks headed back to the warehouses would need to be off-loaded onto docks already crowded with pallets of product that would now not be going anywhere. Further complicating the situation, 50% of Dot's business involves refrigerated or frozen food, which must be kept at specific temperatures to maintain its integrity and suitability for consumption.

Simultaneously with all of the returning Dot trucks, trucks from suppliers would be arriving to drop off even more product, product with varying degrees of shelf-life. Dot measures its success, in part, based on "turns" for each slot on each shelf in its warehouse. Some product turns as slowly as three or four times per month. Other product turns daily. Now, product would be sitting on the warehouse shelves indefinitely. Those with a short shelf-life would become obsolete and unfit to be sold within weeks.

Eversman met with his Business Development Managers (BDMs), a well-trained and fairly experienced team. These professionals had worked for years helping food manufacturers understand the benefits of selling their products through Dot instead of directly to food distributers. These managers would now have to call their contacts and ask them to halt delivery of product that was already under contract, the opposite of their normal aim. But return of the product was only one of a number of awkward elements of those conversations.

It had become immediately clear to Dot's leadership that cash flow would slow to a trickle in the coming weeks as customers cancelled orders. Most suppliers were willing to halt their deliveries and cancel existing purchase orders. But the BDMs also had to ask their suppliers for extended payment terms on inventory Dot had already purchased.

Each relationship with a supplier is unique. BDMs would need to think quickly about how to approach each supplier, factoring in what they knew of the supplier's history with Dot. Each BDM had dozens of suppliers to call in a two-to-three-day period. It would put their relationships to the test like never before. Eversman needed to trust his team to figure out how to flex in every conversation.

Building the Right External Relationships

As you've read in other chapters in this book, much of business success and the ability to remain nimble in business requires building the right relationships. Relationships are organic and develop over time. Dot's founders, Robert and Dorothy Tracy, knew this from the start of the company in the fall of 1959.

Robert, or "RT" as he was known by all, had had been managing a dairy in the Midwest at a time when every small town had its own dairy. Most dairies sold not just milk, but related products like ice cream. Those outside the dairy industry are often surprised to learn that to make ice cream, dairies need milk powder as well as milk. Dairies have to buy that milk powder from food manufacturers. As the manager of a dairy, Tracy knew he was tying up substantial amounts of capital in milk powder inventory. He knew this challenge was not unique to him. As a friendly and outgoing leader, he had built relationships broadly across the industry, and understood the financial burdens others were experiencing.

He spotted an opportunity. Tracy quit his job and founded Dot's predecessor company, Associated Dairy. He bought large quantities of milk powder and other products the dairies needed and sold them only the amounts of each product that they needed for the week. The redistribution industry was born.

The company was immediately successful, providing jobs for at first dozens and then hundreds in the local town of Mt. Sterling. While many people find the courage to follow their convictions and start a company, few do so when expecting their eighth child, as the Tracys were. The confidence in your ideas and in your own abilities allows you to tackle challenges others shy away from. The Tracys would go on to have four more children as the company grew. A few decades later, I would meet that eighth child, Mary Tracy, when she worked at Covenant House in New York. I met RT and Dorothy a year later when Mary and I got married.

In the 1980s, local dairies started consolidating. Tracy and his seven sons and five daughters, many of whom were by then working at and helping run the company, recognized that their market was rapidly changing. The number of potential customers was shrinking, and those that remained would not need the company's services as extensively. The company pivoted away from dairies and toward "food service," providing the same redistribution benefits to the restaurant and other food outlets that they had been providing to dairies. To reflect that change in business focus, Associated Dairy Products changed its name to Dot Foods, and then eventually to Dot, which had been Dorothy's nickname in college when the couple met.

The company would pivot repeatedly as they branched out into refrigerated and frozen foods, to restaurant supplies, and to creating an online marketplace. Each expansion required rethinking how they were reaching their market, and deftly taking advantage of the circumstances around them. Most importantly, it required knowing the players in the space, having solid relationships in place, and moving at the right pace.

According to George Eversman, Dot's success at building strong relationships was based on decades of building a spirit of collaboration toward solving the suppliers' problems of getting their product to market. Those relationships paid off that March when the Dot BDMs had to call their suppliers. Many suppliers agreed to work with Dot on a solution that would meet the needs of both parties.

Business relationships are built on mutually beneficial arrangements. We don't often ask for "favors" from our business partners. Covid proved to be a time when businesses had to ask for favors, sometimes lots of favors, and showed many businesses who their strongest partners really are. Relationships, even business relationships, are built on trust. That trust proved crucial in the weeks that followed the initial shutdown.

BELIEVING IN YOUR INFORMATION

Throughout the pandemic, we all grew frustrated with the conflicting information we were hearing, and not just from competing news outlets or those with agendas other than the population's well-being. Sometimes the contradictory information was coming from the same source. The effectiveness of wearing masks, where to get PPE, when and for how long we needed to quarantine – no matter how well intentioned we wanted to be, we couldn't act appropriately if we didn't know whose advice to trust.

Those functions within Dot's business that were at the mercy of outside information were just as hesitant and challenged as the rest of us. Other functions – those that made decisions based on internally sourced data – were in much better shape.

In *The Power of Trust*, mentioned in earlier chapters, Sucher and Gupta note that our competence at achieving our claimed abilities is crucial to building trust.[1] Dot's competence is based, in large part, on how it leverages data. That competence helps the company build trust with its external stakeholders and have confidence internally in its ability to meet its promises.

Dot thrives on data. The company Chairman, Joe Tracy, calls Dot "a technology company that happens work in the food industry." Data impacts every aspect of the company. The operations group talks constantly about the "cost per hundredweight" (CWT), which means the cost of moving 100 pounds of product a single mile. The group knows CWT for any given mile in the United States. Understanding those numbers informs its decisions regarding when and where to build a new distribution center. The company's food safety team monitors the shelf life of the 125,000 products on the shelves of the warehouse. Dot Transportation (DTI), the division of the company that manages the company's fleet of 2,000 tractors and trailers, uses various software to track both the location and the wear and tear on the both the equipment and the drivers.

Confidence in the accuracy of the data on hand allows the company's leaders to make both strategic long-term decisions and to be nimble when those decisions have to be made quickly. "Dot has a long history of investing in technology to manage the business more effectively," days Brian LeDuc, Dot's Chief Information Officer. "Since the 1990s we have electronically tracked specific product and shelf-life attributes down to the exact bin or 'slot' across our 5 million square feet of warehouse space."

Dot's response to the crisis required trust internally as well as with its external partners. Although the BDMs were able to decrease inbound deliveries, Dot still struggled to manage storing the volume of product when the level of outbound deliveries remained uncertain. Throughout 2020, the food service business had shrunk by 60%. Customers were still buying product; the country had to eat. But food distributors couldn't gauge their own needs from week to week. Therefore, they weren't buying product sufficiently in advance to allow Dot to plan well. Decades earlier, Dot had had the foresight to create one of the first and largest food sales websites in the world, which provides a direct real-time connection to their customer needs. That technology gave Dot years of information about individual customer's buying trends. Prior to March 2020, Dot used that information to predict how much product they would need on hand.

Unfortunately, all of that data became meaningless overnight. Models would have to be reconstructed or abandoned, replaced with real-time input from customers, which required more communication. Product sat on shelves, and uncertainty reigned where regiment had previously created stability.

Although the historical data was no longer valuable, the existence of the technology platform itself allowed Dot to be nimble in the moment to respond to the crisis. "Two years before the pandemic, Dot started investing heavily in a data analytics practice," LeDuc noted. When the shutdown happened, LeDuc and his team of 160 IT professionals immediately went to work evaluating every aspect of the business. "We continuously re-evaluated and re-implemented our system rules for ordering, allocating, and reserving product as the landscape shifted. Within weeks we created a new website for our customers and employees to buy heavily discounted overstocked products. Within a few months we had whole new systems for early detection and decision-making for ordering and dispositioning at-risk products."

At the time, Dot had 11 distribution centers across the United States and Canada, mostly based in rural areas. Dot's headquarters is still in its original location of Mt. Sterling, in Brown County, in West Central Illinois, a farming community of 2,000 located about 45 minutes east of the Mississippi River.

Getting product from Burly, Idaho, to Bear, Delaware, is no easy feat. They needed to know where there was space across a vast warehouse network and at the right temperature to house their products safely. Data enabled them to do so.

How to get the product from one place to another is the easy question. The harder question is knowing whether it's worthwhile to do so. That's were knowing your CWT becomes essential. While you may be able to locate space in a warehouse across the country, you need to also know the cost of getting that product to that warehouse. In a business where profits are measured in fractions of cents, you need to have tremendous confidence in the accuracy of your data. According to LeDuc, "We track each order and product as it is received, picked, packed, loaded, and delivered to our 5,000-plus customer locations across the country and internationally. So, we trust the information in our systems and the knowledge we have built over the years." Dot's well-developed tech operations gave them the confidence to make rapid decisions and to remain nimble.

Counting on Internal Relationships

For the sake of perspective, Dot operations will move over $9 billion in food in 2023. Given Dot's reach in the food industry, if you eat out at a restaurant at the same frequency as most Americans, chances are you have eaten food that has passed through a Dot warehouse. By the end of the third week of March 2020, the crisis at the company shifted from an overload in the warehouse to an overload on the psyche of the people involved in keeping the country fed. Within a few weeks of the lockdown, Dot had its external business under control. Now, it needed to manage internal issues. Again, strong relationships were crucial to success.

Solutions to complex problems usually involve many components. The company, still a family-owned business, had never laid off an employee in its 60-year history and didn't plan to do so now. Dot is a "family" business not just a "family-owned" business. Because most of its distribution centers are in small towns and are sizable employers in those towns, many employees at each site are related. It's common for siblings, cousins, and multiple generations of families to work in various parts of the company. Those relationships between employees and between families of employees and the company build trust.

Instead of considering layoffs, Dot's HR and finance teams quickly structured a fairly intricate voluntary furlough program. Enough employees at various levels throughout the company took advantage of the program, helping the company manage expenses. As some elements of the business slowed, Dot moved employees to other roles that needed to be filled. Everyone understood the need to be flexible and buy into the joint effort to recalibrate to a different work environment.

Focusing on employee health and well-being, while always a priority, now moved to center stage. Dot established an "Employee Well-Being Task Force." According to Eversman, an essential element of their conversations was "fairness."

What does "fairness" look like in a company with such diverse roles as warehouse workers, truck drivers, sales professionals, and all of the support and corporate functions of a regular company? While marketing managers and client relationship professionals could work quite well from home, warehouse workers had to be on site, operating forklifts, stacking pallets with various sized boxes, and loading tractor trailers. No matter how much we all tried to adhere to social distancing in the early days of the pandemic, we invariably came into contact with each other. That was true at Dot as well. Given how little was known about Covid in its early days, that contact created anxiety for many.

The truck drivers had an even more difficult time. While they might be alone in the cab of their trucks most of the day, the start and end of every trip meant interacting with people at other companies. The "unknowns" of the disease were now complicated by further "unknowns" of the rules of engagement at the dozen or so companies a driver might interact with in any given week.

In the early days of the pandemic, the CDC expressed how it was working hard to understand how the virus was transmitted between individuals, and how it spread though the body. In the meantime, Dot – and all transportation companies – were moving product throughout the country and the body politic. Doing so safely and with care created a constant concern for the employees.

The risk employees had to expose themselves to varied greatly. Since Dot's warehouses tend to be in small towns, some employees could enjoy their morning coffee in the safety of their kitchens, while watching their colleague-neighbor head off to work at the warehouse. Communication around those issues became crucial, with managers trained on how to help people talk through those frustrations. Because the company works hard to build relationships across the organization and help everyone understand how they are all interconnected, they build trust and engender patience with each other instead of animosity.

Earlier in this chapter, I shared that strong and nimble leaders differentiate between what they can control and what they can't. None of us could control the conflicting health information we received about the pandemic on a daily basis or the changing protocols. We could, however, control how we acted as a result.

Trying their best to follow the ever-evolving guidelines by various government agencies, the Dot HR team would issue new protocols whenever necessary. Since Dot's warehouses are spread across many states, each distribution center had to follow additional regulations unique to their location. Large companies are accustomed to managing operations in multiple states; they just aren't used to the rules in each of those states changing weekly. Being nimble in their responses was crucial.

Although Dot has yet to perform a thorough debrief on its overall Covid response, Eversman offered his own assessment. "I think we did OK on our crisis response. We got through it," he offered. "I think we did really well regarding health and wellness. We really tried to meet people where they were, keeping everyone employed and engaged and safe." He then offered, "Where we could probably have done a better job was at minimizing change. We were trying our best in an ever-evolving landscape, but we may have been *too* nimble with regard to staying on top of policy changes. If we had to do it over again, I think we could have put broader policies in place that would have allowed us to make fewer changes on things like social distancing, masks, quarantining, and other aspects that would have allowed employees to not get whiplash about what they could and couldn't do."

"We tried to be transparent," Eversman said, "but it's hard to do so when you don't know when things will shift again. We thought our decisions would be long-lasting but then the rules would change. We ended lots of announcements about our latest protocol with the line, '. . .for now,' knowing these rules were likely to change. We could have included that caveat more consistently."

Dot, like most companies, has dealt with its share of challenges. The difference with Covid, according to Eversman, was the severity and immediacy of the crisis. "We've had to factor economic downturns into our strategic plan before, but you usually have months of warning to evaluate the situation. With Covid, the downturn was far more significant than we had ever experienced, and it happened without warning."

ACT

RT and Dorothy Tracy were comfortable taking decisions forward. As their company grew, they needed to trust the judgment of others to make decisions as well.

In his book *Call Sign CHAOS*, former Secretary of Defense James Mattis shares his leadership style. He advocates that leaders should set the tone, set the objectives, make sure everyone is on board, and then give your people the freedom and authority to make decisions in the moment.[2] While managing a food redistribution company in crisis is not on the same scale as leading marines into battle into Afghanistan, the same leadership approaches apply.

According to Eversman, the lynchpins of making it through the first two weeks of the crisis were flexibility and nimbleness. The collaboration among diverse disciplines required a creativity and openness beyond the norm. As this new joint team met regularly, Eversman realized, "Pretty frequently, my best move was to just stay out of the way." He noted, "You need to trust the people on your team to be able to do their jobs well. I realized I was asking people to explain to me what they were already doing, and then instructing them to do it. I was just slowing down the process." The people closest to the situation were the ones best able to identify a solution to the problem. "My job was to give them the information I had about how much inventory was coming into and out of Mt. Sterling and letting them fix the problem." Eversman was just one more conduit of information that shared the necessary data with the right teams to allow everyone to make clear decisions.

In prior chapters, we discussed the Innovator's DNA. The fourth element of being innovative is "experimenting." Separately, in Chapter 5, we looked at the idea of "fast fail," being willing to try something new but not let the experiment go on for too long. Experimenting requires taking action. "Calculating" the risk involved means being confident in your information. That minimizes the number of fast fails and increases your likelihood of "sudden successes."

Three times per year, the 25 top leaders at Dot meet for a four-day Strategic Planning Meeting to revise the company's one-, three-, and five-year plans. Starting in the fall of 2020, the group met four times just in the course of a few months trying to assess the food business landscape and prepare how the company would need to restructure, refocus, and remodel its operations.

"We had serious questions about whether the food industry would ever be the same," Eversman noted. "Would people ever go out to eat again with the same safety lens? I was convinced salad bars at grocery stores would *never* come back."

He noted, "We had to ask ourselves, 'What does the company need to look like to be successful going forward?' and 'What do we need to do differently in order to succeed?'"

The company started developing contingency plans for a variety of scenarios. Many of those scenarios played out right in front of them as 2020 wore on. They saw some food distributors close for good. Other entities consolidated. New opportunities arose. Efficiencies emerged. According to Eversman, "Now, the food industry doesn't look that much different than it did pre-pandemic. It shows how resilient people are and how sound concepts endure."

Although Dot didn't have to face a completely reconstituted food industry, it did gain knowledge and wisdom from the many scenarios it considered. The company learned some great lessons.

According to Eversman, "We all got better at making faster decisions. At Dot, we have tons of data that guide our decisions. During Covid, we had to make decisions faster. You have to trust your instincts, even knowing some of your decisions will be wrong. A fast, adequate decision was better than a slow, really good decision."

They also learned not all decisions needed to be made. "Because we got good at making decisions faster," Eversman notes, "we made more of them, which sometimes frustrated employees. Overall, making faster decisions is a net plus. We could have been more thoughtful regarding whether all the decisions we made actually needed to be made, or if some of the decisions could have waited."

Some environments are fluid, and some are whitewater rapids. The decisions that Dot's management had to make during the pandemic required fast thinking and fast action. Although the time frame on making those decisions and taking those actions was condensed, the need to refocus efforts and reassess business models was as old as the company itself. Dot had done so repeatedly as it grew from a dairy-supply company to a food service redistributor to a technology company that happens to be in the food business. Each successful pivot required reliance on relationships built over time, an accurate assessment of the quality of data being received, and the confidence and bravery to move forward.

TAKEAWAYS

Being nimble in times of stress requires the confidence in your stakeholder relationships, leveraging the information available, and having the guts to move forward.

I have coached hundreds of senior leaders as they prepare to deliver presentations at their organization's strategic planning meetings, similar to the regular meetings at Dot. Almost all of the discussion is about some broad market data, internal information, and questions for colleagues about their take on current trends. Rarely have I seen anyone spend any significant time thinking about, articulating, and challenging themselves regarding the strength of their stakeholder relationships.

A company's risk assessment discussion might include an evaluation of key buyers' economic viability should the market turn, or a calculation of amounts due on long-term contracts. But the conversation rarely goes beyond that. In this new age of change, perhaps we should extend that discussion to include the level of confidence we place in our suppliers and buyers to stand with us as true partners, invested in each other's success.

With data, sometimes "more" is just "more," not "better." For data to be useful and a net gain for your operations, you need tools for interpreting it. If you are still looking at a long-used report and shrugging, "That data is problematic," or "We all know that data isn't reliable," you're compromising your ability to be nimble when the next crisis occurs.

Finally, assess your leadership approach overall. Do you empower people to make decisions and then trust them when they do so? Where are the bottlenecks in the decision process? Those bottlenecks choke the organization. To be more nimble, we need to breath.

Questions for you and your team to consider:

1. At the time of the Covid lockdown, what did we perceive were the most immediate threats to our organization? Were those, in fact, the most immediate threats? Were there other priorities that we should have identified and dealt with first?

2. At the start of the pandemic, all businesses needed help from their stakeholders – their customers, their suppliers, the entities that support and enable their business. What did we learn about the business relationships we had cultivated over the years? How did others reach out to us and how did we to them? Were our relationships strengthened or diminished?

3. What data is important to us? How does having that data allow us to make faster, more informed decisions in times of crisis or when quick shifts in approach are needed? How can we obtain that data?

4. Do we trust our team members to make the right decisions in the heat of the moment? Have we created the right atmosphere of independent thought and decision-making that would allow people to solve problems well and by themselves, or have we created a team that simply follows orders?

CHAPTER 8

Get It Done

September 18, 1787 – Philadelphia

Question from Ms. Powel: *Sir, what have we, a republic or a monarchy?*

Benjamin Franklin: *A republic, if you can keep it.*[1]

We've looked at being nimble in the face of unexpected challenges at work. Let's take that discussion one step further and assess what being nimble looks like in the face of a true, immediate crisis or national emergency.

Being nimble is about getting comfortable with uncertainty and responding effectively to change when it happens. When change occurs in one area of our lives, we try to maintain the greatest amount of consistency in the other areas. In times of upheaval, if we are nimble at handling the immediate threat to normalcy, we can hang on to whatever consistency we can, which gives us comfort.

Democratic governments exist to provide the stability that allows individuals and organizations to function. The U.S. government has been a symbol of stability for the world for more than 100 years. The democratic process can be clunky and often messy, with arguments, hidden motives, and compromises. But we count on the process itself to work. Sometimes we get lulled into believing that the process exists on its own and is self-enforcing. On January 6, 2021, we learned that the process only exists and functions to the extent we make it do so. It works because we make it work.

On January 6, during the attempt to undermine the certification of the 2020 presidential election, thousands of people worked to keep the process of democracy on track, as many others sought to dismantle it. For most of us, being nimble in the moment allows us to accomplish our small tasks in our own narrow world and of little consequence beyond ourselves. But on January 6, the small actions of the moment would impact not only the nation, but history. For some, on January 6, being nimble required an understanding of one's skills, one's purpose, and one's role in the democratic process.

In much of this book, we have looked at how organizations or industries have responded to disruptions in the marketplace or sudden changes to their business model. Organizations function through the actions of individuals. While history books will analyze the response of political bodies and law enforcement on January 6, I thought it would be helpful to look at the actions of a single individual caught up in the middle of the melee. Assessing how being nimble helped him through a day of dangerous encounters and desperate actions may provide a plan of escape for each of us if we ever face that level of urgency ourselves.

PROFILE: U.S. HOUSE CHAMBER ON JANUARY 6, 2021 (GOVERNANCE) – ONE PERSPECTIVE

Early Morning

On the morning of January 6, 2021, among the other chaos in Washington, D.C., a bomb scare forced the evacuation of an apartment building on C Street N.E. Tom Suozzi, the then

U.S. Congressman representing New York's 3rd Congressional District on Long Island, lived on the second floor. He had planned to head to the Capitol later in the afternoon when the vote to certify the election of Joe Biden as president was scheduled to take place. The bomb scare, one of many that day in D.C., changed his plans, and he headed out earlier than expected. He planned to spend time at his office in the House Cannon Office Building, just to the south of the Capitol, but that was also closed because of a bomb threat. Instead, he entered the Longworth House Office Building next door. On his way up the steps of the building, he could see and hear the growing clamor coming from the crowds in front of the east side of the Capitol building.

He took the tunnel that runs from the House office buildings under Independence Avenue and to the basement of the Capitol. Because of Covid restrictions, access to the floor of the House chamber was restricted to those participating in the debates, which meant, mainly, Republicans. Suozzi took the elevator straight to the third floor, which opened near the hallway outside the House chamber gallery. In the hallway, he saw Capitol police looking through the third-floor window at the mob that had gathered on the west side of the building far below. As he entered the gallery, he heard them comment on how large and loud the mob was getting.

The "gallery" is the balcony that runs the entire perimeter of the House chamber. Down below, on the main floor of the chamber, are two notable locations. First, there are the large double doors at the back of the room where presidents enter when they deliver the State of the Union address. Second, there is the large dais from where the president speaks, and where the vice president and speaker of the House sit during that annual event. It's from this multi-tiered dais, called the "rostrum," that the speaker presides.

The part of the gallery above the rostrum is reserved for the press, and so is closed off from the rest of the balcony. By the time Suozzi arrived, about 30 other members of Congress were seated throughout the gallery. Suozzi chose a seat above and to the left of the Speaker's rostrum, close to the press box, and settled in to listen to the debates.

As the crowds outside the building grew bigger, Suozzi started getting texts from his wife, Helene, who, like the rest of the country, was watching the event unfold on TV. Her texts were more curious than anxious at the time, just asking about what was going on and if he was aware of the growing mob. Like the rest of us, she did not expect that the demonstration would turn violent, and the Capitol would be breached. "I kept assuring her everything was OK and that I was in the chamber," Suozzi said. "I told her to keep me posted on what's going on outside because I didn't have access to TV."

Early Afternoon

From his seat in the balcony, Suozzi had a clear view across the chamber to the double doors where the House sargeant at arms announces the arrival of the president once a year. Just below and to the left of him were those lawmakers and aides on the rostrum. On either side of the rostrum are doors leading out to the Speaker's Lobby, a long, elegant hall decorated with the portraits of past speakers of the House.

"I watched the proceedings for about an hour when all of sudden, Nancy Pelosi's security detail rushed her off the floor and out the doors into the Speaker's Lobby. Immediately, Steny Hoyer, the House majority leader, was whisked away as well. We still weren't sure what was going on at that point," Suozzi recounted.

Representative Jim McGovern, the chairman of the House Rules Committee, restarted the proceedings, but, immediately, a Capitol police officer took to the dais and announced that the Capitol had been breached and that tear gas was being used in the Rotunda. Suozzi recounts, "He informed us, to the surprise of many, that there were gas masks under our seats, and then he instructed us on how to rip open the black plastic bag and retrieve the masks. He told us they would be escorting us immediately from the chamber."

The session was gaveled into recess. Then things started moving very quickly.

As Capitol police started evacuating the members from the floor, Suozzi recalled, "We could hear a 'Pop! Pop! Pop!' coming from the doors where the president enters. I thought it was gunfire, but it turned out to be a CO_2-fired piston that the mob was using to break the glass in the doors and gain access to the House chamber. The Capitol police, guns drawn, had been joined by two lawmakers to barricade the main door to the chamber. There are no stairs from the gallery down to the chamber floor within the room." Suozzi said, "I was trying to figure out how to get down on the floor of the chamber to help them barricade the door, but there was no way to drop down from the balcony safely, and they didn't need an injured Congressman to add to their list of troubles."

Congressman Jason Crow (D) of Colorado's 6th Congressional District, a former Army Ranger, was also up in the gallery, about 10 yards away from Suozzi. "Crow yelled over to me to check the door behind me to make sure it was locked, and the mob couldn't get in, so I start climbing over chairs carrying my gas mask to check the doors. I had no idea what I was going to do to secure them, but in moments like that you just start to do something." Fortunately, the doors were locked, which provided at least the veneer of protection.

The Capitol police evacuated those lawmakers and their staff on the main floor of the chamber by taking them out the doors behind the rostrum into the Speaker's Lobby, down the stairs to the left and to safety. But those in the gallery were trapped. The mob was pounding on the gallery doors in the back of the room, and it was unclear what other exits, if any, were safe.

For 20 minutes the lawmakers huddled in between the rows of seats, not sure what would happen next. Then, they all heard the gunshot from out behind the rostrum when rioter Ashli Babbitt was shot by Capitol police as she climbed through a window into the Speaker's Lobby. "That sound was unmistakable," Suozzi recalled. "Immediately you could hear all of the Capitol police radios start peeling, 'Shots fired in the Capitol! Shots fired in the Capitol!' and someone shouted, 'Everyone down!' That's when people got down on the floor and tried to figure out what to do next." With the crowd trying to break through the doors beneath them and the doors behind them, and the chaos in the Speaker's Lobby across from them, it became apparent to all of the lawmakers in the gallery that they were surrounded.

Suozzi's seat in the gallery was at the farthest point from any viable exit. He traveled the entire circumference of the room to be in the best position to exit when the time was right. Ultimately, he knew he just needed to keep moving and that sitting still wasn't going to help.

Suozzi knew they needed a strategy. Once the immediate needs were addressed – gas mask and immediate safety – they would need to find a way out.

"The doors were locked and there was nothing else we could do to improve that situation," Suozzi recounts. "So, I started thinking about 'what next?' Would we have to figure out a way to all jump down from the gallery to the floor of the chamber? Was that even feasible? Would they even be safer there? There were more than two dozen of us stuck up there, and at least one member was walking with a cane because of recent knee surgery. Various scenarios were playing through my head, as I'm sure they were for everyone else up there.

"I had been in Congress for four years at that point. For 15 years before that, I had been in an executive function as the mayor of Glen Cove and then as county executive for Nassau County on Long Island. I had been the one making the decisions rather than pushing legislation. My instinct is to act, not sit still. We just didn't have any information on which to make decisions. We didn't know who might be behind any door."

According to Suozzi, Nassau County has the eleventh largest police department in the country. "From my time as their supervisor, I knew I shouldn't try to run this situation; I should leave it to the professionals."

After Babbitt was shot, the rioters trying to break into the Speaker's Lobby started to back down, and the Capitol Police were able to secure that space. At the same time, they secured the hallway outside the gallery. "They led us out the south side of the chamber and to the right," Suozzi recounted. "As we turned left to descend the stairs to the basement, over to the right we could see a dozen or so rioters face down on the floor, with their hands behind their backs secured with zip-tie handcuffs."

They went down the stairs to the basement and to a space that had been predesignated as a "secure location."

Evening into Morning

It took a few hours for various law enforcement agencies to clear the Capitol of rioters. During that time, Suozzi was focused on one goal – returning to work to finalize the certification of the election. "It just kept running through my head," Suozzi remembers, "'We have to get back. We have to get it done.' I knew the main focus would need to be that we needed to certify the vote. We couldn't let the American people wake up the next morning and not have closure on this."

Although security wanted the lawmakers and their staff to stay put in the secure location, a number of lawmakers, including Suozzi, returned to their offices. "I kept the lights off so people outside wouldn't know I was there, but I needed to be somewhere I could think and contact people." His chief executive instincts started to get the better of him.

"I went back to the Capitol to find out what was going on. I was stepping over broken glass and pieces of furniture. There were puddles of liquid on the floor which I think were the residue from the tear gas canisters. The whole thing was surreal. I found the Chief of House Administration, the team that runs the building and entire complex. I started asking what I could do to help get things restarted so we could return to work." Suozzi recounted, "I had lost sight of how big an operation this all is. There were thousands of people involved and only a handful making decisions, and I was limited in terms of what I could accomplish." He returned to his office to await news.

In the end, of course, Congress returned to work that evening and certified the election of Joe Biden as president in the very early morning hours the next day. While we are still learning the details of the events of the day and the complicity of those involved, the lessons from that moment are clear. We no longer live in a world where we can take our democracy for granted. Had the rioters entered the House chamber or actually come into contact with any of the lawmakers, there's no telling if the certification would have taken place. For the first time in our history, there was no peaceful transfer of power.

When the rules we thought were written in concrete were apparently only written in our conviction to uphold them, we need new guidelines by which to make decisions. We need to know our own parameters for behavior.

Where Nimble Comes In

According to Suozzi, there are three elements to making decisions in times of crisis.

"First, you have to know what you want – the end goal you want to achieve." In the case of the January 6 insurrection, there were two goals: first, provide security for self and others, and second, certify the election.

"Second you have to have the guts to try to make that change happen because there will be people who don't want the change you're seeking. They will fight you to maintain the status quo." On January 6, those opposing forces were first, the rioters, and second, the lawmakers who wanted to stop the certification. While pure survival instinct may have provided the courage to deal with the first challenge, it was a commitment to the U.S. Constitution and the Rule of Law that drove the commitment to meet the second challenge.

We don't need to be nimble in times of calm. We need to be nimble when matters are urgent. While in the chamber, Suozzi knew that time was of the essence and that he needed to act. He didn't know how he was going to barricade the door, but he knew he had to solve the problem, not hide behind a chair.

Once security had been restored, he needed to find a way to be helpful. While actually moving the process forward was beyond his control, he kept looking for a way to make that happen. Going back to the Capitol in the evening and seeing the scope of the damage was his way of gathering information and perspective, and seeing if there was a way to help.

"Finally, you have to know how to win. You need a plan that makes sense." Creating that plan in real time requires listening to the right voices. Suozzi had no combat training. Like most members of Congress, he doesn't normally find himself in life-threatening situations, and hadn't expected to do so that day.

Surrounded by rioters and with the sound of gunfire nearby, Suozzi and the others in the gallery that day were experiencing sensory overload. In times like that, we don't need more information; we need to be able to sort the important information from the clutter. As Suozzi was looking over the railing of the gallery trying to figure out a way to lower himself to the House floor to help secure the door, he heard his colleague Rep. Crow, the former Army Ranger, telling him to secure the doors behind him. Knowing that Crow had experience in battle that he himself lacked, he chose to listen to better advice and secure the door. Acting on the voice of experience instead of the instinct of the novice helped secure the room and likely spared him a broken bone or two if he had jumped down to the chamber floor.

While the plan for getting out of the House chamber was rightly left to the security forces, the plan for completing the certification was provided by the Constitution. It just took a lot more effort than usual to carry it out.

Values Lead the Way

Suozzi notes, "All of those elements are driven by your values. When times are tough, in the end, you can't rely on other people. Your family, your friends, your colleagues – they will each have things in their lives that influence them that you can't control. The only thing you can rely on completely is your set of values.

They will never abandon you. You still have to make difficult decisions, but those decisions are easier to make if you know your values. In that way, we create our own stability."

For Suozzi, the aftermath of the incident was to decide if he could ever work with his colleague across the aisle again. He notes, "Most of us will not be faced with being under siege, or working in close quarters with colleagues who may have instigated the siege. But you have a job that has to get done, so you work with people. You're there to do a job."

Although most of us will never feel the strain of confronting an angry mob, it's common for many of us to feel a siege mentality at work. Very often, we need to make decisions on key issues that significantly impact the lives of other people and the health of our organizations. There are always competing interests at play.

As someone who led a small company for more than a decade, I know the pressure I faced when I had to fire someone from the organization and make that call on a very short time frame. I was aware of the impact my decision would have on that person's livelihood and ability to support their family. I weighed that against the impact on the integrity of the organization and the blowback I would receive whichever path I chose. It wasn't an easy decision. However, I knew my end goal – safeguarding the business. I had the authority to make the decision, and I was confident the company could survive any repercussions of the decision. Because I also knew my own values and those of my firm, I was able to make the tough calls. In the end, we need to keep moving forward.

TAKEAWAYS

The events at the Capitol on January 6, 2021, are a prime example of leaders needing to ensure stability and continuity in a historic moment of unexpected turmoil. As with most complex situations, the outcome was determined not by the actions of one person, but by the concerted action of many, all making decisions in the moment and with limited information. Even through the vantage point of one person, we see the actions of many playing out.

Paying attention to those whose experience we trust, staying focused on a goal, and having the strength to move toward that goal and with a solid plan to achieve it combine to allow us to be nimble when needed, even in a crisis.

Questions for you and your team to consider:

1. The "peaceful transfer of power" that is a hallmark of our democracy is, in a way, the "business continuity" plan for our nation. What does "business continuity" mean to us? What does our continued existence as an organization mean to our clients or customers? What does it enable them to do? What do we provide that makes us valuable to those we serve?

2. What does "courage" look like for our organization? How do we articulate that for our team so they can show up every day feeling empowered?

3. Does our organization's culture allow people with competing views to continue working together smoothly after disagreements? How do we facilitate moving past damaged relationships to keep the organization moving forward?

Chapter 9

See the Opportunity

It's kind of fun to do the impossible.

—*Walt Disney*

Being nimble requires intentionality. When we pivot, whether when playing a sport, planning a vacation, or pursuing a target client, we're conscious in that moment that we are shifting our direction, our focus, or our strategy. If you're on the basketball court, when you sidestep an oncoming opponent, the action itself is reflexive, but your frame of reference of being ready to move is conscious and requires a heightened level of mental presence. You're mindful of your place, your role, and your objective.

When circumstances require us to shift, to find a new way, our reactions can fall into one of three categories.

1. We freeze. The very idea of change takes us by surprise.

2. We cope. We muddle through with a fatalist attitude as if the optimum outcome is simply our survival.

3. We refocus. We look for an opportunity to grow.

We can prepare ourselves for the next change coming our way through practicality and practice. Step 1: Accept that change is inevitable. Step 2: Build muscle memory for taking advantage of opportunities.

Saving the National Basketball Association (NBA) for last in this book was a slam dunk decision because the NBA's business model, its team nature, and its ethos all drive toward winning.

Profile: The NBA (Sports and Social Responsibility) – Where Opportunities Abound

The first moment when many people in the United States realized that Covid would be a game-changer for us all was on March 11, 2020, when it literally changed a game. According to news reports,[1] 10 minutes before the Utah Jazz were scheduled to play the Oklahoma City Thunder in what was then the Chesapeake Energy Arena, Oklahoma Governor Kevin Stitt received a call saying that a Jazz player tested positive for Covid. Coincidentally, Stitt happened to be at the arena for the game. He met with Clay Bennett, the Thunder's owner, and they called Adam Silver, the NBA Commissioner, to understand the league's policy on this type of matter. Silver, in reply, asked the governor for Oklahoma's policy. Within minutes, Silver decided to suspend not just the game, but the entire 2019–2020 season.

The league, like many organizations, then spent a few weeks in limbo, not sure what the next days or weeks would bring, but then quickly had to figure out a plan. Or not. Playing basketball games is not the equivalent of providing healthcare. The world can survive without a basketball season. But the NBA's mission is: "To inspire and connect people everywhere through the power of basketball." During the pandemic, the world needed inspiration, and during lockdown, we certainly needed a way to connect. That meant the league's only option was to figure out how to get back on the court.

According to Kelly Flatow, the NBA's executive vice president and head of the Events Group, the NBA's mission statement isn't just a platitude; it's a guiding star. Basketball is unique in the world of sports because of its flexibility and its democratic nature. "You can play it in urban or rural areas, with any number of people, and without a lot of planning. It's what makes it a great game." It is the most accessible of sports. "When the league shut down in March that year, we all had no idea what we were going to do, but we knew we would do something," she recalls. Her confidence wasn't just the result of her natural exuberance. It was borne of her experience seeing the league respond with grit and determination to address other challenges, including all of the work done by the league's Office of Social Responsibility.

When the season was suspended, the league's 30 teams had played between 63 and 67 games each. In a normal season, each team would play 82 regular games – 41 at home and 41 away – followed by playoff games.

Figuring out a way to restart the season fell on the shoulders of Byron Spruell, NBA President of League Operations. While the world waited for daily updates on social distancing requirements and other protocols, Spruell, Flatow, and their team strategized how they might help the leagues' teams practice, and, ultimately, compete.

At the NBA, the teams aren't the only ones practicing daily. The C-Suite at the NBA includes, in addition to the usual Chief People Officer and General Counsel roles, a President of Social Responsibility & Player Programs, an Executive Vice President of Global Events, and my personal favorite, a Chief Fan Officer. (How many of us would love to need a Chief Fan Officer for our companies?) The organization's leadership has a long history of promoting innovation.

The NBA's youth basketball program is in a constant state of evolution, helping kids develop not only foundational basketball skills but creating guidelines for kids' overall health and wellness. The league's social outreach arm, NBA Cares, has created more than 2,000 play spaces for kids in 40 countries, each one tailored to the needs of the community in which it operates. In fact, "Innovate with Intention" is one of the NBA's four core values. As a result, while the NBA was caught off guard by Covid like the rest of us, they were more practiced than most at being nimble in their response.

The league also has a long history of activism, where it also remains nimble as needs arise. For years leading up to the pandemic, NBA Cares had been involved in a variety of social justice initiatives and criminal justice reforms through its support of the Vera Institute of Justice. On Friday, March 13, 2020, the same day as the lockdown, Breonna Taylor was killed by Louisville, Kentucky police when they fired 32 shots into her apartment. Her death prompted weeks of protests, all part of the burgeoning Black Lives Matter movement. Some NBA players wore her name and face on T-shirts, and the NBA referenced her in public service announcements during games. The protests and the engagement of players in racial justice initiatives would expand dramatically after the murder of George Floyd two months later.

Putting a Plan in Place

On June 4, the league approved the following plan for getting back on the court. Twenty-two of the league's 30 teams would be invited to restart the season.[2] Each team would need to coordinate individual workouts for its players at its home facility. During July, all players would travel to Florida, to what would become known as the "NBA Bubble." The Bubble was a quarantined enclave consisting of three Disney resorts in Bay Lake, Orlando, and the ESPN Wide Worlds of Sports Complex nearby.

"As we were planning this," recalls Flatow, "one of the first people I called for advice was General Martin Dempsey. Dempsey had been the chairman of the Joint Chiefs of Staff and had recently been appointed chairman of U.S.A. Basketball. "I asked him, 'What sage advice do you have for me?' He replied, 'In every crisis there is an opportunity.' And that certainly was true with Covid and with the move to the Bubble."

According to Flatow, "When we made the decision to go into the Bubble, Florida had one of the lowest incidents of Covid. By the time my team and I landed there to set up, around June 19, it had one of the highest rates. I remember talking to the team and saying, 'OK. We're just going to have to take this one day at a time.'" Her acceptance of the fact that she was going to have to be nimble in the moment was, in itself, being nimble. There was no resistance. There was only recognition that we live in a fluid environment.

Once on site, each team would play another eight regular season games at the Complex. The result of those games would determine the playoff schedule. Everyone would follow strict Covid protocols. No one would leave the quarantined areas, including the NBA staff. In total, 1,400 people lived inside the Bubble for 110 days, including Flatow and her team of about 100. No such operation had ever been tried before. The Bubble was creative problem-solving at its finest.

"Every day was a new adventure," Flatow recalls, highlighting that it's not normal to live for three months straight with all of your co-workers. "You never knew what was going to be the issue of the day, but you knew every day you were going to learn something new – new about your role, new about your colleagues, new about your own abilities." Flatow shares her memory about that time not with disgust or despair, but with a matter-of-factness that conveys she understands what it takes to be nimble. Knowing she would be learning on so many levels kept her open to shifting, to seeing possibilities, and to taking advantage of opportunities.

Flatow has spent 17 years contributing her marketing and communications know-how to solving problems for the NBA. According to her, the NBA has a culture of innovation. "We're always game to try something new, which is good. Sometimes I think my first 15 years trying new things with the NBA was all just the practice and drills for what happened at the Bubble." In those early days in the Bubble, *everything* was new.

She highlights that the corporate organization of the NBA takes its cues from the sport itself. "You're a team. You have to listen to each other, respect each other's talents, and collaborate." Many of the players and others were skeptical about how and whether the whole experiment would work. "And we struggled sometimes, particularly in those first few weeks. We failed a lot, and when we did, it was all over social media." As someone with great depth in the world of media relations, she knew how quick, nimble responses to challenges were important. "Everyone has always had their own narrative in life. It's only recently that those narratives have a platform for being shared."

She recalls the first challenge, and one that arose almost immediately, concerned the food at the resorts. "We hadn't paid enough attention to what it takes to feed hundreds of elite athletes," Flatow recalls. "When you have a captive audience, and you're telling people they can't leave the Bubble, you need to feed them really well."

It's not surprising that food became the first on-site challenge Flatow and her team had to address. In psychology, there's a time-tested concept known as Maslow's Hierarchy of Needs,[3] which defines how we prioritize what we seek, starting with our physiological needs, which include air, water, and food, up to our self-actualization needs, which is defined as "the desire to be the best we can be." Arguably, NBA players have already achieved the highest level in Maslow's pyramid. They have achieved the pinnacle in their profession. For anyone accustomed to meeting that level of psychological need, to be lacking one of the lower levels of need is a shock to the system.

Flatow notes, "The players and staff weren't being picky or acting entitled. But when you're not sure how long you're going to be stuck in a place, you suddenly realize you'll need to make the best of your situation, and good food goes a long way toward making people feel comfortable and cared for." She notes, "The staff at the resorts were terrific. They got right on it, and everyone noticed the improvement immediately."

Flatow has been in the business for more than two decades. "The speed of change is what's most noticeable to me. When we talk about having to pivot, it's not in terms of days or weeks. It's now in terms of moments. And inside the Bubble that continued to be true," Flatow recalls. "Nothing was normal in those days," she notes. "It wasn't normal for us to be away from home for so long and living in isolation. Life in the pandemic wasn't normal for anyone on the planet. We felt that if we could get the season restarted, we could give people some normalcy, and that might help people cope."

Being nimble in the Bubble meant coming up with new ideas and being willing to try new approaches every day. While televising the games helped fans at home feel some sense of return to normal, the teams were playing to empty arenas, with camera crews too busy working to cheer and applaud. Flatow and her team installed 17-foot-wide monitors in the stands with rotating live images of actual fans watching the games remotely. "It wasn't perfect, but it brought an energy to the game that had been lacking," Flatow noted.

"What plays into our success," she notes, "is understanding that we don't have all the answers all the time, and that listening to people is incredibly important. We're very fortunate. We've got incredible players and coaches, equipment managers and communication specialists. And everyone actually listens to each other."

"We were doing something that had never been done before," Flatow notes. "There's this Disney quote that became our mantra. 'It's kind of fun to do the impossible.' And it felt like we were doing the impossible every day. It seemed daunting at first, but every day we iterated and made improvements, and each day got better."

The "regular" season games, if they can be called that, wrapped up in early August, and on August 17, the playoffs began. By then, if not a well-oiled machine, things in the Bubble had settled into at least the semblance of a routine.

ROUTINES ARE MEANT TO BE BROKEN

Although being in the Bubble meant isolation from people on the outside, it didn't insulate those on the inside from other social and political events. As noted above, for months, demonstrations had been raging across the country protesting the police shootings of Black men and women. The Black Lives Matter movement was helping build awareness more broadly about both police brutality toward people of color and about the challenges Black Americans, in particular, face when dealing with law enforcement.

In response, in early August, the NBA established the NBA Foundation, committed to "Driving economic empowerment and opportunity in the Black community." One of its signature projects is the All-Star Pitch Competition, giving young Black entrepreneurs the chance to showcase their ideas. Initial funding for the foundation came from a 10-year, $300-million commitment that all 30 teams agreed to support. The players knew the teams and the league were willing to invest in needed reforms. More than money would be needed.

Then, on August 23, in Kenosha, Wisconsin, police shot Jacob Blake seven times in the back while arresting him based on a 911 call reporting domestic violence. The shooting prompted demonstrations across the country. Two days later, on August 25, demonstrators in Kenosha were confronted by counterdemonstrators. Kyle Rittenhouse, a 17-year-old, shot three of the demonstrators, killing two of them.[4] Further protests ensued.

In the Bubble, players' frustration was mounting. On August 26, the Milwaukee Bucks boycotted Game 5 of its series against the Orlando Magic as a sign of support for protesters and frustration with continued racial injustice. As a result, the league postponed all games for the day as the NBA and the National Basketball Players Association (NBPA) discussed how they could help with racial justice reforms.

Flatow recalls the reaction from NBA leadership. "We have always been an organization that prioritizes listening. We value different points of view and understand that the social aspects of what makes the game great is also what allows us to have impact more broadly." In response to the Bucks's decision, NBA leadership thought it would be helpful to give the players a chance to talk about these issues in a safe environment. Obviously, players on many teams, not just the Bucks, were upset about what was happening. Basketball players are public figures with standing in their communities. They have a presence on social media and know they are able to influence a public conversation.

Flatow and others wanted to provide the players a chance to come together across team lines and share their concerns, their own experiences, and their ideas.

"So, I get a call in the middle of the afternoon saying, 'Can you find a space where we can bring all of the players together safely for a conversation this evening?' My team and I had been in Orlando for more than two months already, and every day had had its own challenge. But figuring out this was a whopper." The largest room on the campus was a ballroom at the Coronado Springs Hotel. "We scrambled to help the staff create groups of seats spread out enough to meet protocols, but close enough to allow for an intimate conversation among the players. I distinctly remember being in there with my team and the Disney Cast Members[5] wiping down everything with Clorox wipes. Then, we brought all the players who wanted to participate in for a conversation, and we got out of the way."

Being nimble requires being willing to pitch in when needed, no matter what the task. "At the NBA," Flatow notes, "there's no such thing as staying in your lane." She emphasizes how in the Bubble, they were in constant "create, test, rejigger, discard, and start over again," mode. "We had no choice but to try new things, new ways of talking to each other, of dealing with each other, and of succeeding together. Because we take our cues from the game, we remain nimble and figure out a way to score."

"I wasn't in the conversations, so I don't know exactly what was said, but there was a clear sense based on what came out of that room that the players thought they could accomplish more together than individually. They wanted to use their influence not as individual stars, but as a community." The conversations that day took place with players from all of the teams present, all in one space, and on very short notice. The meeting, the conversation, the momentum, would not have happened had the players not all been together in the Bubble. Flatow didn't know it at the time, but her team on the ground was leveraging an opportunity provided by one tragedy to create a response to another.

The conversation in the Coronado ballroom sparked ideas for both short-term and long-term opportunities for the players to take a stand, or a knee, on the racial and social justice issues facing the country. "Black Lives Matter" appeared in large letters not just on the T-shirts worn by the players during warmups and when seated on the bench, but on the floor of all official basketball courts being used for play. Players were allowed to replace their own names on the back of their jersey with a meaningful message of their choice about social justice and racial equality.

The impact of that conversation would last well beyond the Bubble. Within weeks, the NBA and NBPA formed the National Basketball Social Justice Coalition, whose mission is to "advance social justice and dismantle systemic racial inequality." They defined three areas of focus – voting rights, policing, and criminal justice reform. And they acted quickly. One of the coalition's first steps concerned voting rights. For the 2020 election, the league opened its arenas as voting venues and shortly thereafter decided the league would no longer hold games on election days starting with the 2022 election.

"Improving access to voting is such a powerful accomplishment, and we're so proud of helping that happen," Flatow notes. "That huge accomplishment was born out of a conversation that was born out of a team's reaction, which was born out of a crisis. Listen, react, move quickly. Make sure people know that they're being heard, and that you are asking what we can do differently. It's about being committed to always improving." The coalition continues to work toward its goal of "Turning People Power into Public Policy."

MOVING FORWARD

The playoffs resumed on August 29 and concluded on October 11, when the Los Angeles Lakers beat the Miami Heat.

Creating and executing on the Bubble was a gamble, but one that paid off. It cost the NBA more than $150 million to design, coordinate, and execute the experience in the Bubble. The league recouped an estimated $1.5 billion as a result of the resumed season. "While the impact of the Bubble was deeply felt by the teams and the organization, you could feel the immediate impact on so many other people in such a time of chaos," Flatow notes. "The Disney Cast Members were always expressing their gratitude to us. Because of the Bubble, they had jobs and could support their families at a time when all of the other resorts were closed." That in itself was a huge accomplishment.

That fact that so many players from so many teams were together at a pivotal moment in the country's ongoing struggle for racial justice was fortuitous. The ability of Flatow's team to make the event happen was the result of its ability to see an opportunity and scramble to make it happen.

Flatow reflects on what enabled her team to be nimble and creative in the face of a crazy amount of newness. "I am fortunate to be in a role where I have to collaborate perhaps more than anybody else in the organization. To do what I do every day requires pulling together communications and social responsibility and security and finance and legal and global partnerships, and every aspect of the league basketball operations to be able to understand what's important to everyone. That's the only way we're able to put our game on a global stage." Flatow believes she and her team can accomplish this because of practice.

"Innovation is in the DNA of the NBA," she says. "Because we listen to our fans, we've been able to bring them into every aspect of the game, from what we are doing in our community programs to our Basketball without Borders program, which we do on four continents every year. We listen to our fans and our constituents, and we design experiences that resonate for them. That's true for our All-Star Games as much as it is for pulling a lot of chairs in a circle so that players can share challenges after a crisis. We can do all of this because we practice being nimble every day."

TAKEAWAYS

We don't suddenly become nimble. It's a learned skill and attitude. It takes practice to build the kind of muscle memory needed to be nimble when the time requires.

If you build that skill set, you can enjoy doing the impossible.

Questions for you and your team to consider:

1. How practiced are we at being flexible and creative? Where do opportunities to practice arise in our business life?

2. How well structured are we to respond quickly to take advantage of opportunities as they arise? What changes would we need to make to move more quickly?

3. How well are our roles and your own psyche structured to allow us to move quickly? What changes would we need to make in our role and in ourselves to be better poised to take advantage of opportunities when they present themselves?

CONCLUSION

We humans are complicated beings. While we all claim to crave independence, we also seek to link ourselves to others, sacrificing some of that freedom. While we espouse wanting to do things our own way, we also jump at the latest trends and fashions. While we are attracted to the new and different, we recognize our need for stability. Providing that stability is the challenge before us as leaders.

It would be easy to say that we are facing times of unprecedented instability, but that's not true. The world has never been settled. It has just seemed calm on the surface for quite a while, and we forgot how chaotic things can get. Nevertheless, we're in a period of uncertainty now and need to lead ourselves and our teams through it. The good news is: if we learn to be more nimble in our responses, we can restore some balance for ourselves and our teams.

To respond effectively to the vagaries of the moment, you need confidence in your ideas, in yourself, and in your team. And your team needs confidence in you.

The stories included in this book were culled from dozens of conversations I have had with business leaders over the last few years. I selected those stories I thought would highlight the messages I heard most frequently regarding how leaders have managed to deal with one crisis after another.

First, to regain our footing and provide that solid support for others, we can start by knowing ourselves.

The team at Covenant House knows that its mission is to keep its doors open for young people in need. The gravitational pull of that core objective gives the place and its people stability.

Bowery Farming makes decisions with confidence and fosters security among its ranks by staying true to its four key values: Opt In, Think Wildly Different, Break Barriers Together, and Be Kind to the Core.

Memorial Health managed through the greatest health crisis of the last few generations by knowing its limits and by focusing on what it could control.

Following the lead of those profiled in the first three chapters can provide you with the solid base on which to then pivot as needed.

Second, we can approach the world with the humility and openness needed to listen and learn, and with the generosity of spirit to share that knowledge with others.

Like Matt van Geldere in the fast-moving world of technology, we're more likely to be open to new opportunities as they present themselves if we approach the world with the humility that allows us to learn.

The insight Julie Lamm provides to her clients and internally at PwC comes from living on a two-way street of information. In every conversation, she shares what she knows and listens to gain more wisdom. That constant growth mindset prepares her for the change just over the horizon.

Most leaders are open to learning to achieve their business objectives. For the team at Salve, helping others learn *is* the objective. When your job is simply to impart knowledge, asking good questions and challenging ideas in the moment helps you craft better decisions and guide your students and your organization through the storms.

Third, we need to act. Being nimble implies we need to keep moving. Balance is both a noun – something we achieve – and a verb – something we do. To balance ourselves, we stay in constant motion. Being nimble means staying light on your feet and always ready to move. If we gather and process the right information, we can move spryly and land securely.

Moving – and moving other things – is what Dot Foods does best. Its employees are comfortable making tough decisions because they have the confidence of their convictions and the data to support their conclusions.

Of all the challenges to our norms, none is more unsettling than violence. Most of us are not accustomed to being attacked, either physically or verbally. Staying calm in a crisis such as the January 6 insurrection requires having a clear objective and the guts to move toward it regardless of the threat.

Finally, rarely do opportunities arrive announced and labeled as such. We need to practice in order to see them for what they are. At the NBA, opportunities to practice being nimble abound. As a result, the organization's nimbleness allows it to spot opportunities. Not a bad reinforcing cycle.

Everyone's situation is unique. Covenant House can't operate the way the NBA does, and Salve can't move at the speed of fintech. You and your organization can, however, learn from these examples. The next challenge to our sense of self and feeling of stability will happen sooner than we expect. The questions at the end of each chapter can guide you and your colleagues as you explore, identify, and clarify your path to becoming a more agile organization. Get ready to pivot. We're in the New Nimble . . . at least for now.

ACKNOWLEDGMENTS

This book, like most endeavors, is a collective effort. I am eternally grateful to the many professionals who have shared with me the stories of how they have remained creative, determined, and, yes, nimble, in dealing with the flood of change that now is our world.

The team that guided Covenant House through the pandemic – Deirdre Cronin, Sr. Nancy Downing, Alison Kear, and Renee Trincanello, and so many others, thanks for all you do to keep kids safe.

Caralyn Cooley, it's been a pleasure getting to know you through this process and to experience the great energy and enthusiasm you have for finding ways to feed the world.

Jay Roszhart, the feats you and your team achieved during the pandemic were astounding. Thank you for your foresight that allowed you to be better prepared than many, and the ingenuity you showed in helping your community deal with such crisis.

Matt van Geldere, your commitment to helping others grow and find fulfillment in their jobs is inspiring. Thanks for being the everyday hero to so many.

Julia Lamm, your focus and insights are tremendous. Your openness to sharing your perspective is a testament to how you help build trust in the business community.

It's been a pleasure working with the leadership team at Salve. Nancy Schreiber, Jim Ludes, and Jim Fowler, your dedication to your profession, the discernment you apply to your decisions, and the constant good humor in the face of challenges provide great life lessons for all.

Brian LeDuc and George Eversman of Dot Foods – I'm not a numbers or a tech person, so I thank God every day that someone else is. Your ability to dive into minutia while keeping any eye on long-term strategy is truly impressive. Thanks for sharing your thoughts with me, and now so many others.

The Hon. Thomas Suozzi, you fight the good fight. You always have. Thank you for being part of the larger effort that helps our democracy move forward.

Brandon Gassaway and Kelly Flatow – like this book, life is a collective effort. You bring people together because that's when the fun happens, and that's when life happens. Thanks for bringing us inside the NBA Bubble and helping us see what premier teamwork looks like.

Sandra Sucher and Shalene Gupta, I've learned a tremendous amount about trust from our conversations, from hearing your talks, and from reading your book. Thank you for turning research into actionable ideas on how relationships actually work.

Wendy Fried of Wordcraft and of three-houses-up-the-street – your insights into and challenges about my writing have helped me grow as a professional and as a person. Thank you. This book makes our collaboration 3-for-3. I'll be in touch about that novel soon.

Thank you to the team at Wiley – Zach Schisgal, Kristi Bennett, Sangeetha Suresh, Jozette Moses, and Barbara Long. Your thoughtful editing, gentle coaching, creative design work, and most importantly, endless patience, have helped bring this project to fruition.

Finally, and most importantly, huge thanks to my wife, Mary. You have spent countless hours alone watching *The Mandalorian*, or reading, or helping plan three weddings at once, while I wrote this book. Know that I am eternally grateful. You are my inspiration in all I do. Thirty-two years together and every day new and exciting. I love being nimble with you.

ABOUT THE AUTHOR

Jay Sullivan is the former managing partner of Exec|Comm, LLC, a communications consulting firm. For 25 years as a coach and teacher, he has helped thousands of professionals improve how they manage and lead their teams. He is an award-winning author and columnist, and was an adjunct professor at Georgetown Law Center and Fordham University School of Law. His book, *Simply Said: Communicating Better at Work and Beyond*, was released by John Wiley & Sons in 2016, and has since been translated into Arabic, Chinese, French, Korean, and Russian. As a contributing writer for Forbes.com and The Business of Law Digest, Jay brings relevant and timely advice on how we can all enhance our communication and leadership skills.

Jay received his J.D. from Fordham University in 1989. That year, he was named among the first class of Skadden Fellows by the Skadden Foundation. For two years, he served as in-house legal counsel at Covenant House, a crisis shelter for runaway and homeless teenagers. He then practiced corporate law for seven years.

After graduating from Boston College in 1984, Jay spent two years in the Jesuit International Volunteer Corps teaching English and helping run an orphanage. His book about that experience, *Raising Gentle Men: Lives at the Orphanage Edge*, was named the 2014 Best Book by a Small Publisher by the Catholic Press Association. Jay sits on the Board of Trustees of Salve Regina University. He and his wife, Mary, live in Pleasantville, New York, where they raised their four children, and in Middletown, Rhode Island.

Notes

Chapter 1: Know Yourself (And Let Others Know You, Too)

1. Jeff Dyer, Hal Gregersen, and Clayton M. Christensen, *The Innovator's DNA: Mastering the Five Skills of Disruptive Innovators* (Harvard Business Press, 2019).

Chapter 3: Accept Your Limits

1. The Innovator's DNA.
2. Forty-four percent of nurses reported experiencing physical violence and 68% reported experiencing verbal abuse during the Covid-19 pandemic, https://www.aha.org/fact-sheets/2022-06-07-fact-sheet-workplace-violence-and-intimidation-and-need-federal-legislative

Chapter 4: Think Beyond Yourself

1. Sandra Sucher and Shalene Gupta, *The Power of Trust: How Companies Built It, Lose It, Regain It*, Public Affairs (Hatchette Book Group, 2021), p. 15.
2. Ibid., p. 17.
3. Ibid., p. 68.
4. Ibid., p. 55.
5. Aristotle, *Nicomachean Ethics*, Book 8.
6. Kevin Simler and Robin Hanson, *The Elephant in the Brain: Hidden Motives in Everyday Life* (Oxford University Press, 2018).

Chapter 5: Learn What Others Value

1. Sucher and Gupta, *The Power of Trust*.
2. See Chapter 5 for a discussion of the "fast-fail" approach.
3. Robert Chen, *Selling Your Expertise: The Mindset, Strategies, and Tactics of Successful Rainmakers* (New York: Wiley, 2022).
4. Ibid., p. 23.

Chapter 6: Seek "Meaningful Knowledge"

1. https://hechingerreport.org/college-students-predicted-to-fall-by-more-than-15-after-the-year-2025/
2. Even Stanford's website struggles to explain that motto.
3. The university does not have data on any correlation between how long someone watched a particular video and whether they applied for that program.
4. I'm discounting *Finnegan's Wake*, Joyce's most ambitious novel, because it is wholly unintelligible to everyone but Joyce's inner demons.

Chapter 7: Keep It Moving

1. Sucher and Gupta, *The Power of Trust*, p. 29.
2. Jim Mattis and Bing West, *Call Sign "Chaos": Learning to Lead* (Random House, 2019), p. 45.

Chapter 8: Get It Done

1. From the diary of James McHenry, Maryland Delegate to the Constitutional Convention, James McHenry papers, 1777–1832, University of Michigan William L. Clements Library.

CHAPTER 9: SEE THE OPPORTUNITY

1. https://www.youtube.com/watch?v=efu4YZUKHIM
2. Eight teams, which would become known as the "Delete Eight," were not invited to participate since their performance in the season put them out of contention for the playoffs.
3. Abraham Maslow was an American psychologist who developed the Hierarchy of Needs to explain how we all approach our lives. The five levels of needs are: Physiological/Safety/Love and Belonging/Esteem/Self-Actualization.
4. Rittenhouse was later found not guilty of murder and other charges. The jury determined he had been acting in self-defense.
5. All staff at Disney properties in Orlando are referred to as "Cast Members."

INDEX